Recording the
GUITAR

John Harris

PC Publishing

PC Publishing
Export House
130 Vale Road
Kent TN9 1SP
UK

Tel 01732 770893
Fax 01732 770268
email pcp@cix.compulink.co.uk
web site http://www.pc-pubs.demon.co.uk

First published 1997

© PC Publishing

ISBN 1 870775 45 7

British Library Cataloguing in Publication Data
A catalogue record for this book is available from the British Library

Printed in Great Britain by Bell and Bain, Glasgow

Contents

Dedication

This book is humbly dedicated to the memory of Alan Murphy, a great guitar player.

1

Introduction

What worries most musicians about recording is the lack of control they have in the studio, and guitarists are no exception. In this chapter we will summarise and attempt to de-mystify the recording process, from setting up, to recording and then mixing. A little knowledge picked up here will go a long way in getting the most out of the other chapters in the book.

The demo

For the demo recording the general process can be quickly summarised. You set up in the studio, record, and then mix. This sounds easy enough – and it can be, provided you have rehearsed, have a well set up guitar, and are reasonably confident. But studio jargon can be confusing for the uninitiated, and nerves in the professional studio can make those self assured fingers turn to jelly on the fretboard! At least in the home studio you don't have the pressures of time and the dreaded 'red light' syndrome to contend with.

The professional recording

While the demo may take only a day or more to record and mix, a professional recording destined for release can take weeks or even months to complete. This may involve recording the same track several times, sometimes with different producers, and also time spent experimenting with different guitar sounds and recording extra guitar parts (overdubbing).

Live versus studio recording

Perhaps the hardest way to record is in concert where you are concerned with getting it right and giving a performance to the audience. At least in the studio you can easily do retakes and patch up any obvious mistakes like bum notes. Yet the difficult thing in the studio session is to recreate the passion and adrenalin of a live performance when you are not in front of an audience. For this reason quite a lot of musicians like to set up and record at least some of the backing live in the studio.

The recording process

Setting up for solo acoustic recording
A room with a good natural sound and two or more good quality microphones on the instrument are needed. If a pickup is fitted to the guitar the output from this is often used too. Extra microphones may be placed in the room at a distance from the performer to pick up the sound of the room's natural acoustic.

Setting up for a band recording
While the set up for a solo recording is relatively simple, the band recording session brings other considerations into play.

Multiple miking
For a quality recording, even if the musicians are all playing in one room, the instruments will be individually miked up. This enables the engineer to have independent control of all the instrument levels and sound at the recording and mixing stages.

Separation
If all the musicians are playing in the same room, sound from the loudest instrument is bound to be picked up on microphones positioned to record something else. This is called 'spill'.

For example, drums (especially snare) down the guitar mic and guitar down the drum mics (chiefly via the drum overhead microphones). Some spill is not a problem, but too much will cause problems later on at the mix. Usually some separation is required and the guitarist may find that the amp is put in a sound proof booth or another room and miked there.

✦ INFO ✦

The guitar will almost definitely need a different EQ (equalisation) from the drums and bass. This could mean a lot of microphones! In a rock session it is usual for the drummer to have seven or eight mics positioned around the kit while the guitarist ends up with one!

Figure 1.1 Band studio set up 1

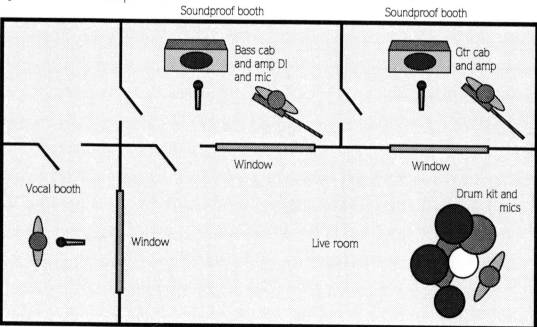

Soundproof booth　　　　Soundproof booth

Bass cab and amp DI and mic

Gtr cab and amp

Window　　　　Window

Vocal booth

Window

Live room

Drum kit and mics

If only one room is available, a DIY approach could involve a home-made screen using sleeping bags or duvet covers to minimise spill. In any case the engineer should make a test recording to check if there is a problem and take the necessary steps to prevent it.

Headphones
If the guitarist is playing in a separate room, headphones (or 'cans') will be needed to hear the rest of the band. This band mix will be fed to the guitarist's headphones via the desk foldback. The engineer will be in control of the individual instrument levels in the mix and the overall volume.

Figure 1.2 Band studio setup 2

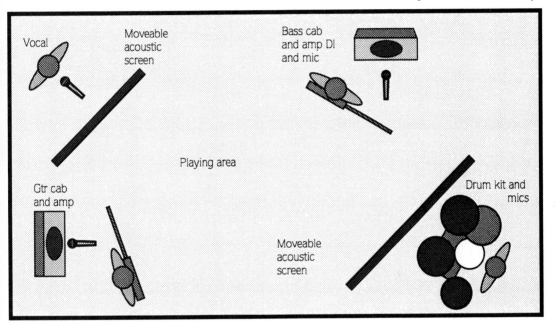

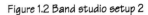

Do not be afraid to call for changes in the level of your headphone mix – ask for more drums or vocal if you can't hear them properly.

In smaller studios you may have to compromise by sharing a headphone mix with another member of the band – I suggest that it's not the drummer, especially if the drummer uses an outrageously loud click track!

A plethora of options!
However you choose to record the guitar sound, a mind boggling set of options is available to today's guitarist. Choice of microphone or DI (direct inject), stereo or mono, live room or dead acoustic, pre-amp, or amp head and cab? And then there's the guitar itself! The type of guitar, strings, plectrum size and pick up you choose – all have an influence on the sound.

Test recording (or, what happened to my sound?)
Once the guitar equipment is in position the first thing you will do is make a test recording to check the record levels and the sound quality. It would

be great if the guitar sound you set up was the one that got recorded and heard on playback. Surprisingly, this is one of the hardest things to achieve in the studio!

Figure 1.3 Headphone mix

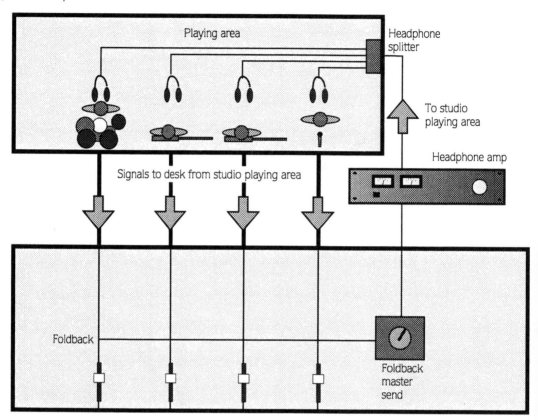

Looking at the simplified signal routing diagram (Figure 1.4) you can see that the guitar signal, whether miked or DI'd, passes through a lot of electronics before it eventually comes back at you through the studio monitors. Each stage has the potential to alter the sound slightly, although in theory they are not supposed to.

Purists will record with as little between the guitar and the recording machine as possible, just using good quality microphones and low noise microphone pre-amps.

Even so, be prepared to work within the limitations of the studio environment. Sometimes a 'natural' sound is not the one that fits with the other instruments. For technical reasons recordings also work best within a limited dynamic range – that is, the extremes of loud and quiet guitar parts tend to be averaged out.

The recording

Once a test recording has been made, a rough instrument balance will be set up using the desk monitor channels. If you are satisfied with the sound you can then proceed to do the proper recorded take! More help is available with this intensive part of the studio process.

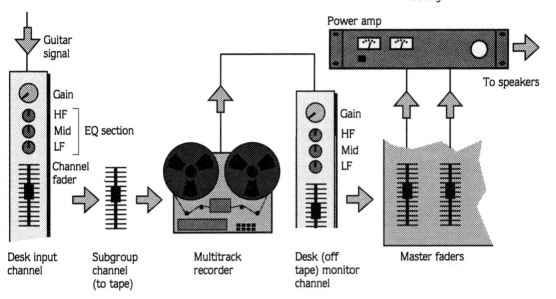

Figure 1.4 Simplified signal routing.

Drop ins

Provided there is sufficient sound isolation (not much spill) you can re do sections of your recorded performance. A good engineer can 'drop' the recording machine into record and out again with split second accuracy to repair a badly played section or a mistake.

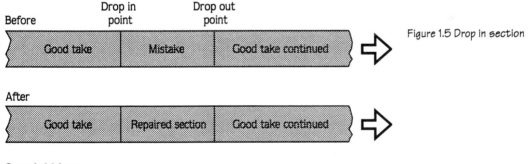

Figure 1.5 Drop in section

Overdubbing

Part of the process of recording may be the building up of a backing bit by bit. The drums may be first, then the bass, then the guitar and so on. Vocals are often added last, although a 'guide' or 'rough' vocal is usually recorded early on in the session. As for 'live' in the studio takes with a whole band you do not have to record rhythm and lead guitar parts in one take. Provided there are tracks available on the multitrack recorder you can record each guitar part separately to a different tape track. This takes some of the heat off in the studio but also makes it easier to mix as each sound has a channel to itself, and therefore can be treated differently. For instance, a lead guitar solo will need to be at a higher level in the mix than a rhythm guitar. You may also want to add some extra guitar parts here and there for a more 'produced' sound.

The mix

When you are happy with the recorded parts you are ready to mix. It is often better to leave this part of the process to another day if you've already spent a lot of time in the studio recording. The engineer will be tired and you yourself can be more objective on another day. Sometimes a monitor or rough mix is useful at this point to check before the final mix.

Mixing can be just as involved and time consuming as recording. In addition to adjusting levels sounds may also need to be equalised and have effects added. In large studios automated mixers can be a great help to the engineer, but in most small studios it's a hands on job for the final mix.

The multitrack recording is usually mixed in stereo to a two track machine and the resulting recording called a two track 'master'. It is not uncommon to mix several versions of one piece of music, each with a slight variation. For example, more or less reverb, the guitars lower or higher in level.

The final two track master will contain all the songs or instrumentals in the correct running order, with the correct gaps between each piece, and with similar EQ and levels. This is called the post production master and is the one that CD's and cassettes will be made from. Naturally, a copy of this is essential as a back up!

Different recording formats

We now have analogue and digital tape, not to mention hard disk systems for recording. But what suits the guitar? An argument rages about analogue and digital which in some ways is similar to the valve vs. transistor debate. All three methods have their advantages and disadvantages.

Analogue

This is a tried and tested format which converts the guitar signal from volts to magnetic energy and stores it on tape. Wider tape formats like 2 inch 24 track give a big sound with a warmth that is very well suited to rock music. Useful side effects like compression and harmonic distortion arise when the tape is saturated by high signal levels.

The down side is that it has a limited dynamic range, and without a noise reduction system it is not ideal for acoustic music. Good noise reduction systems like Dolby S and SR are expensive but can yield excellent results.

Digital tape

Systems like the Alesis ADAT use SVHS tape to store the data in the form of digital code. The advantages are the improved dynamic range of the recording process and the lack of noise from the tape itself. These make it ideal for acoustic music. There is a clarity in the HF (high frequency/treble range) which is missing from the analogue, but it is sometimes said that digital recording lacks warmth. Some of this can be attributed to the quality of the analogue to digital convertors. For rock music you may have to work a bit harder to get a classic 'fat' sound.

Hard disk

Increasingly popular as hard disk prices drop, this is a computer based system with strong powers of data manipulation. The main advantage for guitarists is that you can cut and paste sections of music like a sequencer or word processor can. You may also alter the feel and timing – say from a straight piece to a shuffle at the push of a button. While this might not be 'playing guitar' as we know it there are other advantages to this system.

For example, digital editing may be used to quickly capture the best bits from several takes and seamlessly put them together to achieve one good performance. A great advantage for long classical and other difficult solo pieces. Although this process has been available for years with analogue tape editing, it can be a time consuming process.

Recording at home

Now that the cost of good quality recording equipment has fallen, it is possible to make a release-standard recording at home. One of the main benefits is that you are not paying for studio time, and therefore not worried about how long it takes to get the definitive guitar take. You also have more time to experiment with the guitar sounds and parts. This sounds great, but even a small, fully equipped digital studio is still way above the cost of a decent guitar!

Also on the down side you may have noise restrictions and so can't push the amp and speakers as hard as you'd like; you are unlikely to have access to a good natural live room reverberation; the studio monitoring (speaker and amp playback system) may not be of a high standard; and last but not least, you may be missing out on the skill and advice of a good engineer and producer.

Some of these can be addressed. Guitar pre-amps and speaker simulators are now of high enough quality to be recorded direct, so avoiding the need for a microphone. And artificial reverb, if well chosen, is almost indistinguishable from natural reverb. However, good accurate studio speakers with no tonal colouration don't come cheap, and there's no substitute for a good producer's experience – again expensive!

2

Mixers and signal levels

The signal path diagram in the last chapter shows that all signals go through the desk at least once. This makes it the most important as well as the most impressive looking piece of equipment in the studio. For the guitarist who wants to have a say in the way the guitar recording sounds it is essential to have some understanding of how the desk works.

The mixing desk, also known as the console, is the central control point where signals may be boosted, equalised and routed (studio jargon for directing the path of the signal) to various destinations like the tape machine, two track master, effects units and headphone mix (foldback).

Figure 2.1 The guitar signal can follow several different signal paths.

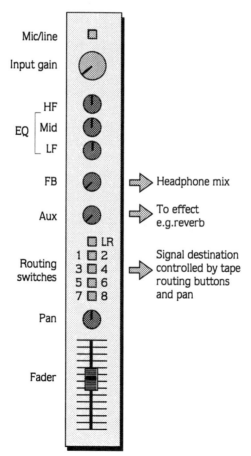

Input gain stage

Mic and line inputs

Because of the wide range of input levels and signal quality, two types of input level sensitivity are found on even the most basic of desks – microphone and line. Without getting too technical, mic inputs are designed to work with the lower level signals that miked up acoustic instruments produce. Even so, most desks can still cope with the high level signals produced by putting a microphone in front of a a cranked up Marshall stack! In such cases on pro consoles a pad switch can adjust the operating range

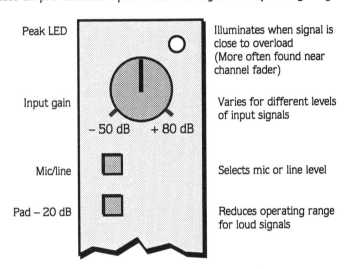

Peak LED	Illuminates when signal is close to overload (More often found near channel fader)
Input gain	Varies for different levels of input signals
– 50 dB + 80 dB	
Mic/line	Selects mic or line level
Pad – 20 dB	Reduces operating range for loud signals

Figure 2. 2 A good input gain section can cope with a variety of signal input levels, from acoustic guitar to a miked up Marshall stack. The gain only deals with one signal at a time – line or mic. Don't be tempted to try both at once – you could damage the channel electronics by overloading the input stage.

by 20 dB or so. Line levels are what you would expect from guitar pre-amp outputs, most effects processors, some amp head DI outputs, keyboards, samplers and drum machines.

Balanced and unbalanced signals

Mic inputs in recording studios use balanced connections while some line inputs may use unbalanced or balanced ones. You can usually tell when a balanced signal is being used because of the tell-tale three pin XLR or stereo jack. A balanced connection uses cunning design circuitry combined with a two signal and one earth path to eliminate noise and interference. This makes it possible to have long cable runs without picking up Radio Vladivostok and avoids the loss of sound quality you would get from a long run of normal, unbalanced guitar lead.

Input signal level

Once you've connected up the signal to the desk you need to adjust the gain. The desk input is a pre-amp gain stage which can alter the input level of the signal on its own channel. A high incoming signal like a miked up Marshall stack needs a low gain. Conversely, a low incoming signal such as a miked up acoustic guitar will need a bit of boosting. In the

Figure 2. 3 Typical guitar
signals using the balanced
microphone input. Some
desks can accept balanced
signals via a 1/4 inch stereo
jack.

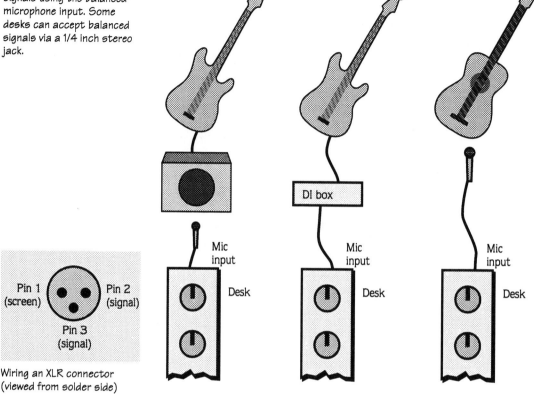

Wiring an XLR connector
(viewed from solder side)

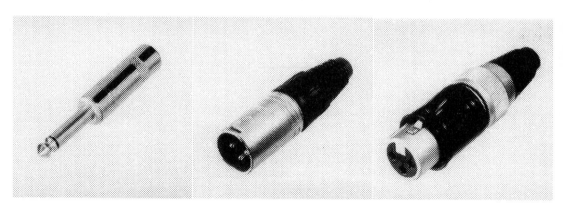

Figure 2.4 Left to right:
Mono jack 1/4 inch (−10dB)
Male XLR connector (+4dB)
Female XLR connector (+4dB)

recording situation the idea is to get as much signal as possible into the channel without overload. This gives you the biggest possible signal level to mask any noise produced by the desk electronics and any other noise. It is what is known as signal/noise ratio and you should bear it mind when using any input stage − for example on a guitar pre-amp or effects units, as well as a desk.

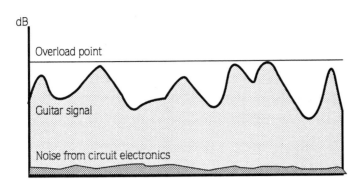

A word about decibels

Decibels, or dB's as they are usually known, are units of measurement in audio. Desks, effects and pre-amps all have them on their input/output meters, and they're even on most domestic cassette players so don't pretend you've never seen them! A decibel is simply a way of expressing the signal level (really in volts) as a ratio. And 0 dB can represent whatever you want it to be for the purposes of establishing a scale.

Let's assume that a 1:1 ratio gives us 0 dB on the desk input meter. For example: If one miked up guitar is plugged into a desk and played at a theoretical fixed level we have a ratio of

1:1 guitarists = 0 dB

Two guitarists playing at the same level yield us a ratio of

2:1 guitarists = +6 dB increase on our desk meter.

In fact on the desk input meter decibel scale (which as you've probably guessed, is not linear) it would take a room full of ten guitarists, all playing at a fixed level to give us an increase of 20 dB, and a veritable concert hall with 100 guitarists to give us an increase of 40 dB!!

As it's impossible to get two guitarists to play at the same level in practice I suppose this is a poor example, but in theory I think you get the point!

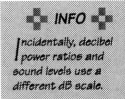

◆ *INFO* ◆
Incidentally, decibel power ratios and sound levels use a different dB scale.

Equalisation

Semi-pro desk EQ usually consists of a treble, bass and sweep mid. Professional EQ will bring in two mid sweeps with a variable bandwidth and more. The bandwidth simply determines how much the range of frequencies on either side of the one you've chosen are affected. Bearing in mind that the guitar operates in the frequency range 80 Hz – 6 kHz it is the mids which will be the most frequently used controls.

Figure 2.6 Typical desk EQ (equalisation). Most channels on a mixing console will have some EQ. The sweep mid frequency control is found on most semi pro consoles now and is the most important for the guitar. While creative use of EQ can completely alter the sound and produce good results, remedial EQ'ing to repair a bad sound can be problematic.

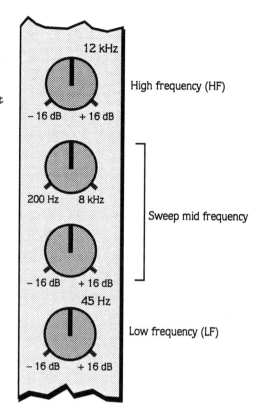

Routing the signal

Auxiliary sends

Auxiliary sends can split and route the signal out of the desk to effects units and foldback. They come in two types: post fade auxiliary send and pre fade auxiliary send.

Post fade auxiliary send

Literally 'after the fader' because the outgoing signal level is also governed by the channel fader level. It is used for sending the guitar signal to effects like reverb or echo. The effects output is in turn connected to dedicated console channels – line inputs or aux. returns. The effects signal can then be routed to tape with the guitar signal or just used for monitoring purposes.

Pre fade auxiliary send

This is the studio equivalent of your independent, on stage foldback mix. Here the performer's foldback is usually on headphones. It is important to hear the other musicians clearly so this headphone mix is crucial. Naturally you don't want any desk channel level changes altering your mix so the aux signal level is pre fade.

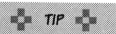

✛ *TIP* ✛

The 'sound at source' school of thought suggests that you should get the guitar sound right to begin with and not have to use desk EQ to compensate for a weak sound source. This is a good rule to follow but in reality a slight tweak of EQ is often necessary in a rushed studio session

Multieffects unit

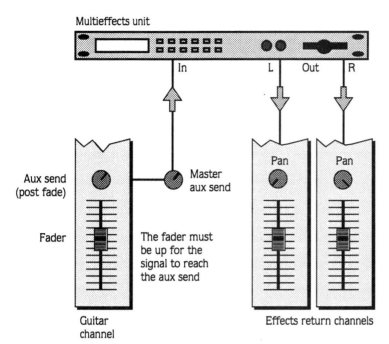

Aux send (post fade)

Fader

The fader must be up for the signal to reach the aux send

Guitar channel

Effects return channels

Figure 2.7 Post fade aux send and return – used for effects. Notice how to give artificial stereo treatment by feeding the stereo effects unit input with a mono signal. The return signals are usually totally effect (wet). These are then mixed against the dry channel to obtain the correct mix of effect and 'dry' guitar signal.

Talkback

For communication between the control room and the playing area a talkback microphone is used. This is often an electret or condenser microphone built into the console itself which can be patched in to the headphone aux mix.

Routing the signal to tape

Signals are sent to the tape machine using direct outputs or sub group outputs. There are two main design types. In line consoles use direct outputs and split consoles have sub groups. Some desks are a hybrid design and give you the option of both methods.

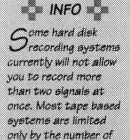

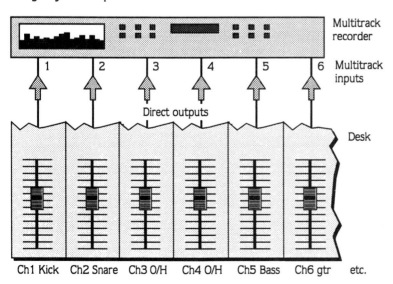

Multitrack recorder

Multitrack inputs

Direct outputs

Desk

Ch1 Kick   Ch2 Snare   Ch3 O/H   Ch4 O/H   Ch5 Bass   Ch6 gtr   etc.

Figure 2.8 Direct output routing to the multitrack. Simple direct routing of signals on desk channels to corresponding recorder tracks. The channel fader controls the level of signal to the multitrack.

Looking at Figure 2.8 you can see that direct outputs can simply link desk channels to corresponding tape tracks. Yet there will be occasions where a guitar signal that is coming into the desk on channel 1, for example, will need to be sent to a different track on the multitrack.

For example, track 1 may have been used for something else, or you may want to double track the guitar you have just recorded on track one. Tape routing buttons allow you to send the signal to the track of your choice on the tape machine.

Figure 2.9 Using tape routing buttons with direct output consoles. Notice how the pan control is used with the routing buttons to determine track designation. To route the guitar to track 2 routing button 1/2 is enabled and the signal panned to the far right. Most desks employ this system to save space.

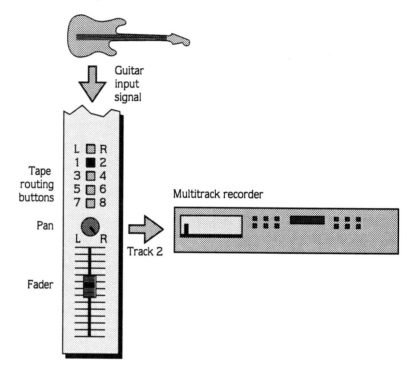

But what if you are short of tracks and want to send two sounds to the same track? Nearly all desk channels have tape routing buttons so two or more signals can be routed to the same destination track on the recorder. This is called sub mixing (see Figures 2.10 and 2.11). An example could be mixing a close miked guitar or cab and a room mic to the same tape track.

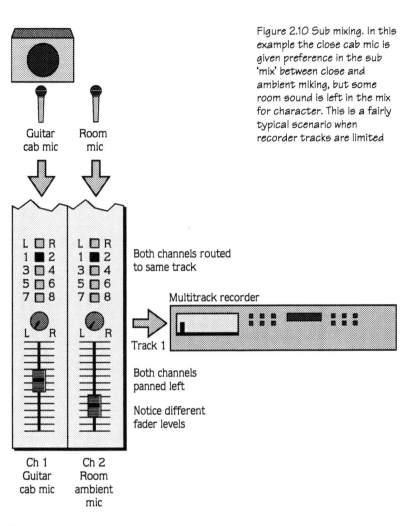

Figure 2.10 Sub mixing. In this example the close cab mic is given preference in the sub 'mix' between close and ambient miking, but some room sound is left in the mix for character. This is a fairly typical scenario when recorder tracks are limited

Off tape listening – playback

In line
Off tape listening (see Figure 2.12) is usually achieved using a set of channels known as the monitor section. Another feature of the in line design is that these off tape monitor channels are built into the same channel strip as the main channel. They offer simpler controls and limited access to EQ and auxiliary sends. It makes for a more compact design but can make it more complicated to follow the signal paths.

Split console
With this design, a completely separate section of the desk is devoted to off tape listening. This often means that it has better EQ and auxiliary access, as well as an easier layout to follow. The downside is that it dramatically increases the desk size.

Figure 2.11 The sub group outputs correspond to the number of tracks on the recorder. Notice that it introduces another set of electronics for the signal to pass through.

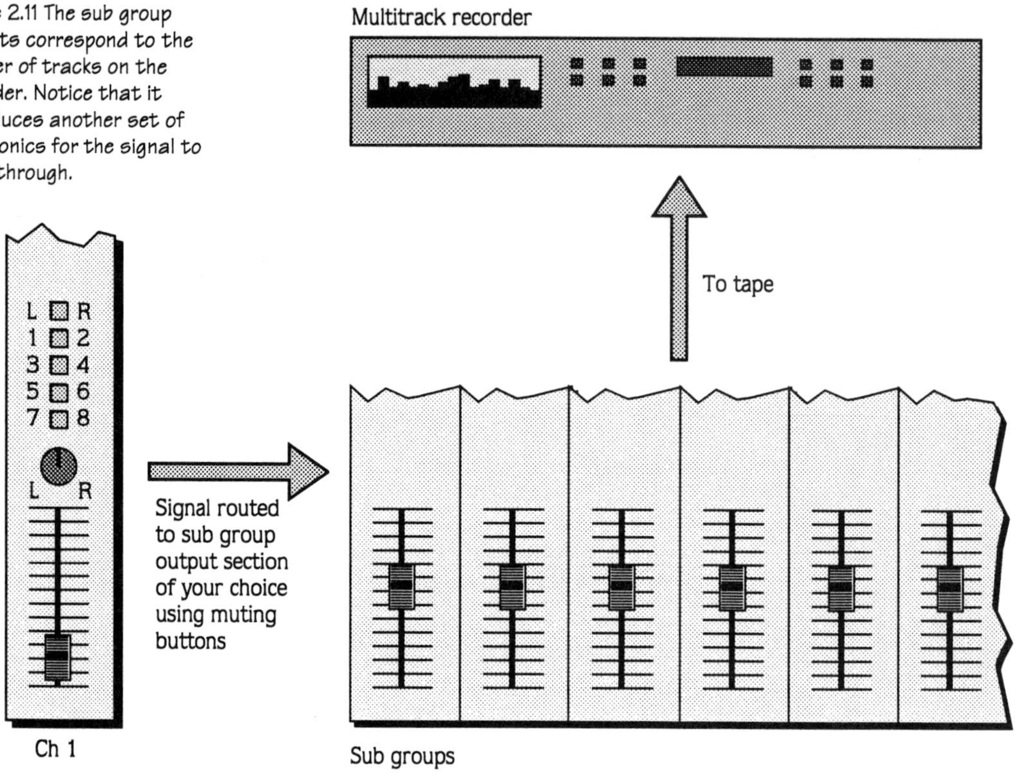

Multitrack recorder

To tape

L ☐ R
1 ☐ 2
3 ☐ 4
5 ☐ 6
7 ☐ 8

L ☐ R

Signal routed to sub group output section of your choice using muting buttons

Ch 1

Sub groups

Mixdown

As we have a whole chapter devoted to mixing later in the book I'll keep this section brief. The mixdown process uses the main channels on the desk for the off tape signals. This takes advantage of the better faders, EQ and auxiliary sends found on these channels. The signal is then mixed to stereo on a two track machine like a DAT recorder. This is your master tape of the session.

On the level

The two main standard operating levels in audio are +4 dB and –10 dB. The better quality of the balanced +4 dB signal makes it the professionals' choice in the studio. You are now probably wondering why it isn't used for all equipment. As far as recording is concerned the cost of better quality cable, plugs and extra electronics soon mount up for so many connections. So a fully balanced system will be found only in a professional studio where there are many long cable runs – a long cable run being far more likely to pick up interference and compromise sound quality.

For the electric guitarist, because of the way pickups and amp heads are designed to interact. a +4 dB balanced signal is unsuitable. However, an amp or pre-amp may provide a quality balanced output purely for recording purposes.

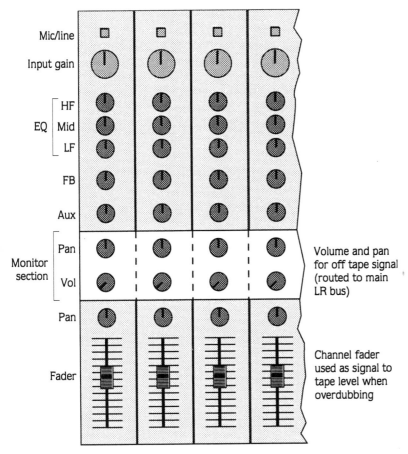

Figure 2.12 In line off tape listening. Note that the monitor channels are on the same strip as the main channel but function, for the most part, independently.. On some desks they can split functions like EQ and aux sends with the main channel.

Mic/line

Input gain

EQ HF
    Mid
    LF

FB

Aux

Monitor section Pan

Vol

Volume and pan for off tape signal (routed to main LR bus)

Pan

Fader

Channel fader used as signal to tape level when overdubbing

Problems will arise when you try to plug a piece of equipment that operates at one level into another. A typical example for guitarists would be when using studio rack mounting effects units with a guitar amp.

Problem 1: The guitar output produces an unbalanced signal of −10 dB or thereabouts. The effects input is looking for +4 dB. It will be hard for the guitar to drive the input of the effects unit hard enough and there will be a worsening of signal to noise ratio by 14 dB. In a nutshell, that's more noise and less signal.

Problem 2: The effects output at +4 dB will overload the amp input which operates at −10 dB.

Fortunately variable level controls have now been introduced on effects units so that they can be used at +4 dB or −10 dB.

Frequency – what is it?

In simple terms frequency has a pitch relationship within the range of human hearing. Low frequencies are in the bass range and high frequencies in the treble range. Let me explain further how this is defined.

When you pluck a guitar string it vibrates, moving from its starting point as far as it's going to go in one direction, back to the starting point and then an equal distance in the other direction. This is called one cycle of movement. The period of repetition of this cycle is measured in seconds and this is what defines the note. For example, bottom E (open string) on the guitar vibrates at approximately 82 cycles per second, referred to as 82 hertz (Hz) and is a measure of the pitch.

Bottom E on the guitar is 82 Hz and top E (twelfth fret)is approximately 660 Hz or 0.6 kHz. Don't get too hung up on the specifications. A good engineer will probably know what the frequencies are but will use his ears rather than check the frequency chart! Incidentally, if you think that 0.6 kHz is rather low, remember that all those nice guitar harmonics give the strings a much higher actual range.

3

Setting up your guitar

Preparation

Some preparation before doing anything important in life is useful. I mean, you wouldn't go out on a hot date before checking how you look would you? Actually I can't think of many musicians who'd swap a hot date for a recording session, but both need some work beforehand! For recording, preparation saves studio time (and therefore money), you get a better sound and you will be remembered for your impressive, professional approach.

Four things are important:

- Equipment maintenance
- Pre production
- Practice
- Mental attitude

Maintenance

Without equipment maintenance you can forget the rest. A guitar that doesn't play in tune, or has faulty electrics will waste precious time. Yet routine maintenance can be carried out by anyone and simple jobs can be accomplished with the minimum of tools. Changing strings, setting intonation and action are relatively straightforward. Truss rod adjustment and fret care should be left to an experienced guitar technician.

Truss rod

Although they rarely need attention, you cannot carry out the simpler tasks like setting the intonation unless the guitar neck and the fretting are correctly set up. The truss rod allows you to adjust the tension of the neck and is found on most guitars. Fortunately you can carry out a quick check of the neck yourself to see if any adjustment is necessary.

Press down the bottom E string at the first fret on the guitar neck (or capo the first fret) and also the fret where the neck meets the body of the guitar. Looking sideways along the neck you should see that the string is not touching the fretboard around the mid point. The neck should be

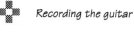

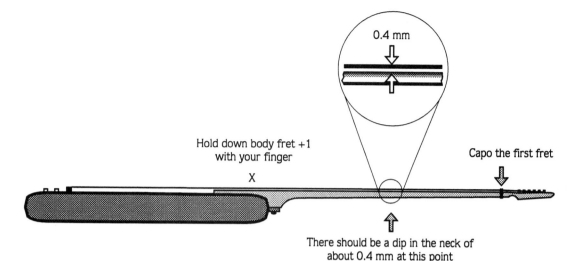

0.4 mm

Hold down body fret +1
with your finger

X

Capo the first fret

There should be a dip in the neck of
about 0.4 mm at this point
(approx seventh fret)

Figure 3.1 Truss rod check

slightly concave. Measure the distance between the string and the fret-board where the distance is greatest. This should be about 0.4 mm, or slightly more for a well adjusted neck.

Changes in temperature, tension and poor guitar care can account for changes in the neck shape. In all but extreme cases, the truss rod can bring it back into shape. Unless you are experienced, take the guitar to a guitar workshop for correction. If you do have a go remember that truss rods are for slight adjustment only!

More dip – 1/8th turn anti clockwise
Less dip – slacken strings first, then 1/8th turn clockwise

Frets

Special tools and skill are needed to fix faulty frets but you can still check out just where there is a problem.

First detune the strings so that the neck is not under tension. Next, fret each string all the way up the fretboard starting from the nut. The first note that doesn't buzz on a string indicates that the fret below it is too high. This is because all the frets should be in a straight line when the neck is not under tension and the higher fret now gives itself away.

New strings

If frets and truss rod are fine you can go ahead and fit new strings so that the intonation and action can be checked. String type affects the recorded sound immensely. Although hybrids exist these are the main types.

Roundwound strings

For electric guitars and flat top acoustics these are the most common strings. The sound is bright and has plenty of attack making it very suitable for many styles of music. The electric strings are made from stainless

❖ INFO ❖

On electric guitars you can get away with some buzz but it will cut sustain. Acoustic guitars cannot afford to buzz or rattle in the studio. Again the remedy is in the hands of a good guitar workshop.

steel and nickel alloy, while acoustic players often favour brass and bronze. Finger squeak can be a problem when playing these strings although some guitarists say that putting a bit of talc on the fingers will solve the problem.

Flatwound strings
No problem with finger squeak here and the brightness is also lost. The resulting mellow tone makes these strings ideally suited for jazz.

Nylon strings
Classical and Flamenco guitars used to use gut but it's now been replaced by nylon, giving a rounded, slightly percussive tone.

Silk and steel strings
The combination of silk and steel give these strings a brighter sound, but they are still not as abrasive on the fingers as roundwound.

String gauge
There are a variety of gauges made up in sets ranging from extra light to heavy. Some guitarists make up their own sets rather than using a standard size.

String characteristics

Light	Heavy
Easier to fret	Harder to fret
Easier to push out of tune	Holds pitch
Easier to bend	Harder to bend
Less volume and sustain	More volume and sustain

If you are a guitarist who plays both lead and rhythm, some sort of mixed set gives you the best of both worlds. For example the Ernie Ball Hybrid Slinky with a light top and a heavy bottom at gauge 009 - 046.

Problems with old strings

Stretching
Old strings become stretched and this can affect the intonation to such an extent that a really old set will not tune up or play in tune across the fretboard.

Dirt
Have you checked under your strings recently? Finger sweat and dirt, smoky bars and poor care will not only make strings dirty, but in extreme cases rusty too! This will affect the vibration and tone of the string. A way to dislodge the dirt is to tug the string firmly and let it snap back.

Cleaning the strings after every gig and rehearsal is another good habit to get into. Some guitarists boil their strings to clean them and then put them back on the guitar. This is a short term measure because the boiling process also makes them more prone to breaking.

More wear and tear

General wear and tear leads to weakness. The flattening of strings on the underside by frets, sharp edges on bridges and saddles, kinks in the string and over tensioning can all lead to broken strings. I even sliced through an old steel string with a copper plectrum once!

When to change the strings

You don't have to change the strings for a recording session but it will help if you are looking for natural presence in the sound. Here are some tips:

- Professionals play in the strings for an hour or so before recording, otherwise they may sound too bright and zingy. Even so, it seems that not all strings need this treatment.
- The technique of tugging new strings about an inch away from the fretboard is a good way to stretch them and stop slipping.
- Make sure that the strings are properly wound onto the machine heads.
- Cut the excess string away on acoustic guitars – the rattle of a tied loop over the headstock can be heard over the microphones.
- For a quick change on a locking tremolo system change the strings one at a time and bring each new one up to pitch as you put it on.

Intonation

To check the intonation you should have a new set of strings on the guitar, tuned up to concert pitch. On each string:

1 Sound the harmonic at the twelfth fret.
2 Fret the note at the twelfth fret.

Both should be the same pitch. If the fretted note is sharp, the scale length is too short and you need to move the saddle away from the nut. If the fretted note is flat move the saddle towards the nut.

Electric guitars with the Gibson Tune O Matic and Fender Strat style bridges have individual saddles. On guitars with floating bridges (mainly semi acoustics) adjust the first E string then the others. Worst off are the acoustic guitars where the fixed bridges allow for no scale length modification. In this case the guitar will need to be taken to a repairer who will re shape or even change the saddle.

String action

Many guitarists think that a low action is the most important thing on a guitar, but it can cause problems. Likewise a guitar with a high action can be virtually unplayable. My advice for the best recorded sound is to tread the middle ground where the guitar is easily playable but the tone is not impaired by a super low action.

Low and high action pros and cons

Low action	
Pros	Cons
Easier to play	Strings rattle
Less effort to play fast runs	Volume reduced
	Tone impaired
	Chords distort
High action	
Pros	Cons
Less string rattle	Harder to fret
Good tone	Barre chords difficult
Louder	

Adjusting the action

Assuming that the frets and truss rod are fine you can go on to alter the action if necessary. Raising or lowering the bridge or saddle adjusts the height of the string. On an acoustic this may involve putting a shim under the bridge saddle or some saddle re design. On an electric either the whole saddle can be moved or individual string height adjustment changed. Usually a screwdriver or Allen key is all that's needed.

There are other ways to adjust the action like tilting a bolted on guitar neck back a little with a shim. Or for more specific problems like a high action on the first few frets the nut may need attention. Invariably this also means that the frets and the neck will need looking at, so such adjustments are best left to an experienced hand!

Equipment maintenance

A footstool, some spare strings and a music stand may be all that the acoustic guitarist brings to the session. For electric guitarists it's not so easy unless a pre-amp is all that's needed!

Checklist

- Check all mains plugs for correct fuse rating and connections.
- Check leads for crackles, interference and breaks.
- Check sockets – loose or worn connections, crackles.
- Check you have spare equipment fuses.
- Valve amp – spare valves.
- Check batteries for active guitars and effects pedals.
- Check for earth hum loops.

Where spares may be needed, make sure that you have them for the session.

Problems with buzz

In the studio, lighting dimmers, equipment racks, fluorescent lighting and computer screens can all cause buzz. It's a particular problem for single coil pick ups and is made worse by poor screening on the guitar itself.

For shielding, use copper foil, a carbon based screening paint or electrical shielding tape. A DIY approach uses aluminium cooking foil but this is not as effective. Make sure that any shielding you use is connected to the guitar earth.

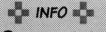

INFO

On one occasion in the studio my amp was in the playing area and the pre-amp in the control room. When they were connected an almighty earth loop started. Yet with both pre-amp and amp in the playing area there was no loop! The problem was found to be that the control room where the pre-amp was plugged in and the playing area where the amp was were on different ring mains. Even such a minor difference in power supply can cause the dreaded hum!

Crackles

Dirty pots and switches can be cleaned with switch cleaner or replaced. Worn jack plugs and duff guitar leads can also cause problems with an intermittent signal or radio interference and need to be changed. Dry joints are another source of crackles but you need to be good at tracing electrical faults to locate and repair these.

Radiated hum

Quite often what you think is an earth hum is being caused by the radiated hum of two transformers in close proximity. This is especially a problem with rack mounted gear where a pre-amp transformer may lie just over an effects unit one. The only answer is to move the equipment in the rack until the problem disappears. External power supplies can also be a source of radiated hum when they are placed next to others or even close to guitar cables.

Earth loops

An earth loop hum is a more difficult problem and can be caused by many things. When two pieces of equipment are individually earthed and you join them together with a guitar lead (which also has an earth – the screen) they can cause a hum at 50 Hz. The safe way of dealing with this is to cut the earth screen at one end of your guitar cable. If you do this mark the cable for future reference as having the earth disconnected.

Do not remove the earth in the plug of one piece of equipment.

Amps

Faulty amps are best left to an engineer, but things like valves can be easily replaced. Tell tale signs that valves are about to go include a loss in level, a characteristic blue glow, or they may become microphonic.

Things *not* to do with amps

- Don't run them with no speaker plugged in – this may damage the output transformer and valves.
- Don't connect an amp speaker output to the input of another amp.
- Don't power up a valve amp without allowing it to warm up first on standby.
- Don't switch an amp on with the volume at 10 and blow your speakers up with the power surge.
- Don't expose valve amps to sudden temperature changes – the valves may crack.

Pre production

This really involves arranging the music, rehearsing it, and choosing what type of sound you need for the guitar part. It really pays to know the music inside out. If you are recording a song it also helps to know the arrangement without the singing, in case the studio vocal foldback is not brilliant.

Session guitar

Session guitarists often need to sight read chord charts or music notation. I have never seen anyone presented with tab in the studio. Even so, if you can find out the key or get a rough mix of the song you are to play on beforehand it will help immensely.

Sounds

Rehearsing the piece doesn't just involve the playing for many guitarists. Nowadays the sound is just as important, so work on that too. If you are using effects, make sure your amp or pre-amp is pre programmed up with the sounds for the session, and also that the sounds you choose are suitable for the material you are going to play. There's little point in trying to play retro sixties or grunge music with a smooth LA session man guitar sound!

Warming up

Before you start playing always warm up. An athlete wouldn't expect to run the 100 metres without getting his muscles loosened up. Start slowly and build up to speed. If you don't, then be prepared for muscle and tendon damage later on in your playing career.

❖ TIP ❖

Provided you have done all these things there's absolutely no reason to lack confidence. Yet nerves can creep up unexpectedly. Everyone deals with them in their own way. Remember that even the best guitarists in the world make mistakes and it's a rare session where everyone in the band gets through a track note perfect.

Figure 3.2 Warm up exercises

Warm up exercise for all fingers - a chromatic scale of A

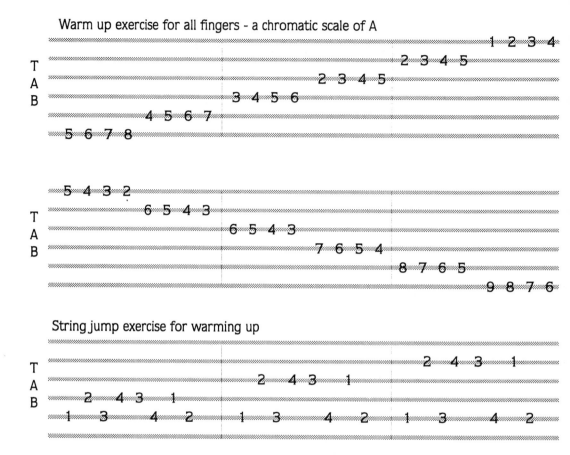

String jump exercise for warming up

These little exercises will help you to use every finger on the fretboard hand and need some astute picking.

4

Miking acoustic guitars

Design and construction

Unlike an electric guitar, each acoustic guitar has its own unique sound, even when it's been factory produced, and this is what makes recording them such a challenge. On an electric guitar the main functions of the wood are to increase sustain and provide a solid construction that the pickups, bridge and other hardware are attached to. So when an electric guitar is played acoustically the tone is bright and thin because on most there is no resonating box to amplify the sound and produce any bass tone. Even on semi acoustics like the famous Gibson 335 the actual size of the chambers are too small to produce anything other than some light mid frequencies.

The acoustic guitar is a different beast altogether. Although there are many types of acoustic guitar – Spanish, Classical, Flamenco and Steel strung, the basic design features have not really altered since the 17th century. The soundbox, strutting, soundboard, saddle and bridge become the crucial contributors to the overall sound. When you play a note on the guitar you cause the string to vibrate and the bridge and saddle transmit that string vibration to the soundboard.

It is the resonance of this soundboard that provides the detail of the guitar's tone, and therefore a lot of attention is paid to the quality of the wood on expensive models – usually a close grained spruce. The soundbox functions as a tuned acoustic chamber which not only projects the sound but provides the crucial bass part of it from the soundhole. The back of the guitar is actually damped by the way you hold it, and so does not contribute greatly to the tone.

Two important things about the acoustic guitar

1 Compared to an amplified instrument it is quiet, so a more sensitive microphone is needed, and you have to be wary of noise problems.
2 Because the whole construction of the instrument contributes to the sound you need to place microphones a distance of a foot or

so away to really appreciate the tone. This in turn can start to introduce the effects of room acoustics as spill. Naturally choice and position of the microphone become critical and there is some argument that the best recording of an acoustic guitar would be made using ambient stereo microphones in an acoustically good room. Yet poor acoustics, lack of good mics and the effects of spill in a group situation could conspire against this choice.

Small room acoustics

If a small room is too 'live', you will find the frequencies that are emphasised are usually in an unpleasant area of the mid range. So miking an
instrument up from a distance in such a room may yield interesting, but
not entirely usable results if an even sound is required.

At the other extreme, the tonality of an instrument is stifled by a dead
acoustic, so you should find that even when close miking in a fairly live
area there is a significant improvement to the sound. A DIY approach
would be to bring in some reflective material like hardboard or plywood
sheets, corrugated metal, even a mirror, then experiment with microphone positions.

Which microphone?

Capacitor and electret microphones are the most widely used for three
reasons:

- Acoustic guitars, especially if they are steel strung, can produce quite a lot of high frequency sparkle which these microphones can capture.
- As I explained, the acoustic guitar is not a loud instrument – compare it to an acoustic saxophone or violin for example! The microphones mentioned have a greater sensitivity to low level signals (remember that they may even be a few feet from the instrument) and can present a workable signal level to the desk input stage.
- The best of these mics have what is known as a flat frequency response. This means that they do not alter the tone of the instrument artificially. Unfortunately they then tend to be on the expensive side.

You can record the guitar with a dynamic microphone but the low level
produced will tempt you to move the microphone closer and so lose its
tonal character. Dynamic mics also can't reproduce the HF. Tandy PZMs
are another cheap option but can give a more noisy and artificial sound.

Noises beeps and spill

The level of noise produced by microphones, cables and consoles is a major consideration when recording solo and group acoustic performances where there is no thrashing rock guitar and hi-hat playing to hide it. Therefore a lot of emphasis is placed on efficient microphones, quality balanced cabling and careful use of desk gain structures to produce quality recordings of acoustic instruments.

One guitarist I recorded finished a gruelling six minute performance and then absent mindedly scratched his chin stubble as the last chord was dying away. Over such sensitive mics it sounded like a chippy sanding a bit of wood! Needless to say that track had a fast fade out when we mixed it!

Shock mount clips for microphones are useful because they don't transfer mic stand vibration directly to the mic, and cushions can solve the problem of tapping feet. Even so, to get around some problems like heavy breathing you may have to reposition the microphone!

Click track

Some guitarists like to work with a metronomic click track which is fed to them on headphones via the desk foldback send. In a solo situation if this is too loud or if the artist is not wearing enclosed headphones it can be heard and spoil the recording. Watch out for it particularly on quiet sections, gaps and fade outs as the guitar sound is dying away. You should really try to deal with this before you actually go for the final recorded take by choosing a metronome sound that isn't too sharp.

If there is still a problem run the click track through a gate so that when the guitar is played the click track is louder and when it is not the click track level drops to the level of the range control – in effect it is following the guitar dynamic. This works on the principle that when the guitar is loud you will not be able to hear the click track.

TIP

You may have other problems with noise too. Beeping digital wristwatches, jangling bracelets, creaking chairs, creaking leather guitar straps, sniffs, belches, grunts and foot tapping can all be produced by the performer, and handsomely picked up by those sensitive microphones! Foot tapping and the odd grunt can sometimes aid the more rootsy recording but most people don't want an ill timed wheeze in the middle of their hardest piece.

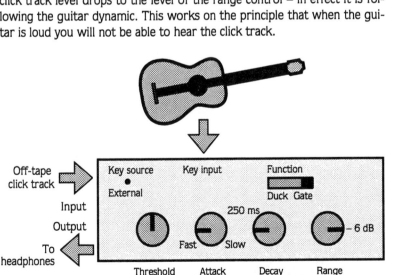

Figure 4.1 Using a noise gate to reduce click track levels during quiet passages in a performance. The guitar signal is connected to the key input and acts as a trigger to open the gate fully. The range control drops the click track signal to a preset level when the guitar is not playing

Finally, if you're recording an amplified band with an acoustic guitarist and you want to use a mic on the acoustic, you'll have to isolate the guitarist in a sound booth. Failing this, only a large room with some sound screens will be enough to keep spill from the other instruments to a minimum. Often a DI signal, if a pickup is available, will be taken as a guide acoustic guitar track. The miked up acoustic can then be dubbed on later in the session.

Number of mics and production considerations

Stereo miking yields a more natural sound (after all we have two ears to listen to the original instrument) but how the acoustic guitar fits in with the rest of the production is also important.

With an electric band

An acoustic guitar mixed in with the other instruments in a band is recorded as a rhythmic texture if it's just strumming along, and the benefits of stereo and natural sound will be wasted, lost among the rest of the sounds.

One microphone should be enough for the job, or perhaps a submix of close miking and ambient mic. Aim for a bright sound and avoid conflict with the bass guitar by avoiding low bass frequencies on the guitar.

Solo performance or break

If the acoustic guitar is on its own, stereo miking would certainly improve the listening experience, and you will need to achieve an even, full bodied sound.

Another scenario could be that the acoustic is featured at the start or middle of a song on its own. Without the benefit of separate tracks to record one full bodied guitar for the breaks and a thinner sound for the rest, you should record the guitar as it should be for the breaks. The bass can be rolled off the other parts in the mix.

Singing and playing at the same time

And why not? Many musicians can give a better performance if they do the vocals at the same time as they play the guitar. In my opinion it is exactly this performance quality that you're trying to capture on tape, and if it causes a few technical headaches then so be it.

Separate microphones for guitar and voice will work, but they sometimes cause phase problems as the guitar spills to the vocal mic and vice versa. A good stereo mic is the expensive option but it's cheaper to use two mics in a stereo configuration to capture both singer and guitar. This relies to some extent on a good acoustic as the mics aren't close in and also a good ear for balancing the mix between guitar and vocal.

Finally you could try a DI on the guitar if it has a pickup, but this doesn't prevent the acoustic guitar spilling to the vocal mic. The distance and position of the microphone(s) are reliant on the relative loudness of the guitar and voice. A good starting point is about 18 inches away, just under head height.

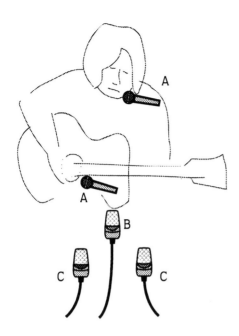

Figure 4.2 Singing and playing guitar at the same time.
A Close mics can cause phase problems as voice spills to guitar mic and vice versa
B One good condenser mic positioned about 18 inches away can work provided neither the vocal nor the guitar sound is compromised. Some compression on the final mix could help
C Two room mics – equidistant from the singer – will sound nice in a good sounding room

Phase considerations and headphones

When using more than one microphone to capture stereo, remember that phase problems will be minimised if the mics are equidistant from the sound source. A quick way to spot potential problems is to wear head-phones and send the microphone signal to them on the foldback. As the player plays and you move the microphones you can clearly hear tonal variation, check for phase cancellation and make a decision on microphone placement. All this without having to run back and forth to the control room to listen over the monitors – can't be bad!

Recording using one microphone

You will find that there are quite a few good positions for miking an acoustic but opposite the sound hole is not often one of them. Although this gives the highest signal level it is also the most boomy because the air vibrating inside the body is designed to give the guitar depth of tone, not definition.

A good place to start is with the microphone about a foot away from the guitar, pointing at the fretboard, around the twelfth fret. This usually gives a good definition of tone. Also listen to each string – one should not really be louder than the other unless played that way. If the tone is still bass heavy try moving the microphone a little further away or further along the fretboard towards the nut. Likewise, if the sound lacks bass, move the mic a little closer to the sound hole. On small bodied guitars it may be necessary to place the microphone closer to the sound hole if you want the extra depth.

INFO

Sometimes slight phasing can be heard on the miked up signal as the guitarist moves in time to the music. This is because the guitar is moving closer and further away from the microphone. Unless it's really bad, don't bother to nail their shoes to the floor!

Figure 4.3 Various ways to close mic the acoustic guitar
A Miking the sound hole will sound bass heavy, but may be more use for small bodied guitars
B Mic at 12th fret, about 9 – 18 inches away is a good starting point, orientating slightly towards sound hole will emphasise strumming and the percussive sound of pick on strings
C Closer to nut 9 – 12 inches away brings out fretting noise, less bass
D Body 9 – 18 inches away emphasises more mid frequencies and resonant 'woody' qualities of guitar
E About 18 inches above the guitar, quite bright, but watch out for heavy breathers!

Fretboard mic

Miking up at the fretboard will give a lighter tone but will also introduce more fret buzz and sliding string squeak. For some players this is an important part of the overall sound.

Miking the body

If you position the microphone on the bridge side of the soundhole you will pick up more of the soundboard resonance and this can sometimes have a harder, more mid frequency sound. It can also sound more 'woody', which is good for earthy sounds like slide guitar.

If your guitarist uses a plectrum, the attack of the plectrum hitting the strings will be emphasised and this is good if you want the acoustic guitar sound to be more percussive, helping to drive the song along. However, because a guitarist's hand will be close to this microphone when playing, it is a good idea to position the microphone out of strumming range and even a little lower than the level of the soundhole on the largest part of the body.

Flamenco guitar can also get a little wild at times and there could be some guitar body percussion involved. The body tapping, sometimes on specially fitted plates, is a high level percussive signal which is often louder than the string sound. If it causes problems you should move the microphone until a good balance between strings and percussion is found.

Dobro guitar will also need a body mic if you want to emphasise the sound of the resonators. However, this is a guitar better recorded in stereo when slide is being used.

Miking from above

It might sound strange, but if you position the microphone about two feet above the soundhole the sound has a nice presence to it, plenty of treble without much bass. This is the perfect sound for placing a guitar in a mix which is quite full already – one with bass guitar and electric guitar, even keyboards. The sound will sit in the mix with no equalisation. The drawback is that the microphone is close to the player's head so any puffs and grunts will be picked up as well!

Mic pointing at the floor

If you want to have more treble edge to the sound and the player is in a room with a hard floor, you could point the microphone at the floor. The high frequency reflections will be accentuated however, so this is a technique better used when you also have a close microphone on the guitar and can mix between the two. The microphone pointing at the floor becomes like a tone control for mixing in more treble.

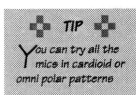

TIP

You can try all the mics in cardioid or omni polar patterns

Recording with two microphones

One close, one ambient. As I just mentioned there is nothing to stop you using one close microphone and one placed in the room. The function of the room microphone is to pick up the sound of the instrument in the room – a sound which is similar to what the audience might hear at a small concert. A nice sounding room is important for this – there's little point putting up an ambient microphone in a room the size of a cupboard, unless you're after a special effect.

The close microphone can be in any of the positions outlined above, but is generally near the twelfth fret or body. The ambient mic should ideally have an open polarity – an omni or figure of eight response to pick up the sound from all around the room, and should be at least five feet away from the guitar.

You can submix both microphones to one track on the tape machine if you are short of tracks, but remember that once committed you cannot remix the balance.

Stereo miking

In most sessions where the guitar is to be the featured instrument or is playing solo, it is worth using two mikes in a stereo configuration. It gives a wider, more expansive and natural sound instead of picking up the sound from just one point on the guitar.

A good starting point is with one microphone near the twelfth fret and one near the body on the opposite side of the sound hole. Remember that the microphones should be equidistant from the guitar to reduce phase problems. The combination of miking close to the nut and near the body also work for some instruments, but as most acoustic guitars have different characteristics be prepared to experiment.

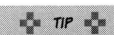

TIP

It is not essential for both the microphones in a stereo pair to be the same model but it does help give a continuity to the sound.

Crossed pair

This is a method of stereo miking where you use two identical microphones at the same distance away, but aimed at different points on the

Figure 4.4 Stereo miking the acoustic guitar
A Twelfth fret and body 9 – 18 inches distance is a good starting point. Mics must be same distance from sound source. Can be cardioid or omni.
B Crossed pair one foot distant also a good starting point
C Room mics are best used in combination with one or two close mics, and in a good sounding room. Make sure they are equidistant from the guitar. Could be 6 – 10 feet away.

guitar. It is a useful way of making sure that phase problems are minimised because the microphones are in approximately the same position.

Ambient stereo

Try an experiment by getting someone to play the guitar. Record the performance and move the microphones a little further away every few bars of music or so. Listening to the playback you may be surprised at the great change in tone and level. The room sound creeps in and eventually dominates. The guitar level falls and there is less bass in the sound. So there are now two things to consider with the sound – tone and level. The room acoustic obviously influences the tone so you must be careful where you put the microphones – should they be near a hard surface, or near a carpeted area?

Carpets and curtains tend to absorb treble and so the sound will have less presence, sometimes a good, sometimes a bad thing. You have to make a decision about the sound of the overall production and whether this guitar fits into this sound picture.

As for level, bearing in mind that an acoustic guitar is not a loud instrument you will have to turn up the microphone input gains on the desk to compensate. Make sure that this does not add unwanted noise.

You should also consider that if your room is not soundproofed the ambient mics will pick up noise from outside, perhaps traffic noise or someone shutting a door. For this reason, the microphones are better when they are held in a microphone 'cradle'. This suspends the microphone in a cradle of rubber bands which do not pass sound wave resonance from the floor and microphone stand directly to the microphone.

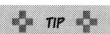
TIP

If you're using two microphones for a natural stereo sound the symmetry should be maintained – if one is over a hard floor then so should the other be. Even so, there are times where you may want to experiment with different room sounds on each mic as a production effect, but this is not standard practice.

More microphones
If you are lucky enough to have more good mics to spare you can try close miking with one or two mics and ambient miking another two. Even so, I'd only really advise this for solo or concert recording.

Polarity
Remember that omni directional microphones sound more natural than directional ones. The possible drawback is that they will pick up more room sound which is not so good if the room acoustic quality is poor.

Specialised acoustic guitar sounds

All of the above miking layouts can be applied to any acoustic guitar, but there are some distinctive designs that warrant extra attention.

Dobro
Developed in the 1920's by the Dopere brothers, the Dobro has a metallic and jangling sound that is louder than the standard acoustic guitar. The vibrations of the strings are transferred to a metal dish or cone. To make the most of the Dobro I'd suggest using two microphones, one to catch the characteristics of the resonator, and the other nearer the neck to reproduce the inevitable slide guitar qualities that this guitar is famous for.

Flamenco
Slightly smaller than the classical guitar the true Flamenco has a brighter and more percussive sound. Tap plates are located above and below the strings on the body for the exciting tapping and striking strokes with the fingers known as 'Golpe' strokes. For recording you have to get the right balance between the hard rhythmic tapping and the actual guitar sound. This could involve using two microphones – one to catch the 'Golpe' strokes and one between the soundhole and the neck for the strings. With one microphone you may have to favour the neck side of the body as the tapping will be a hard transient (fast attack, short release) sound that records as a higher signal level than the strings.

Classical guitar
Classical or Spanish style guitar tends to have a much more mellow sound than steel strung acoustics. Some Flamenco guitarists may prefer the sound for solo pieces. The miking technique is the same as for flat top steel strung acoustics.

Pickups on acoustic instruments

Pickups can be very useful in a live situation but seldom give a true representation of the sound. The simple reason for this is that they pick up the sound from one part of the instrument – often the bridge, yet the tonal character of the instrument is a combination of different resonances best heard at a short distance. Some equalisation can be used to recapture the natural acoustic sound, and this usually involves some modification of the upper mid to high frequencies (a little cut) and the lower mids (again a cut at around 200 – 300 Hz) on stringed instruments.

Figure 4.5 EQ to make acoustic guitar pickups sound more 'natural'

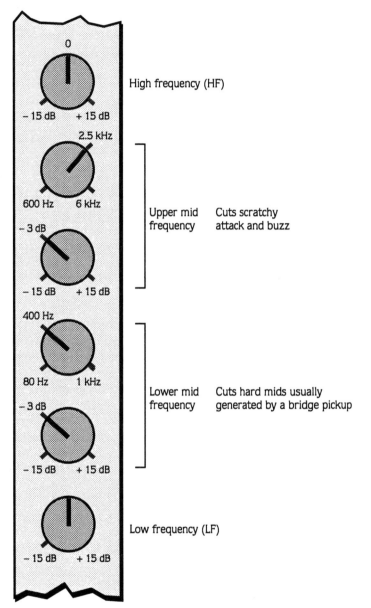

High frequency (HF)

Upper mid frequency — Cuts scratchy attack and buzz

Lower mid frequency — Cuts hard mids usually generated by a bridge pickup

Low frequency (LF)

DI

If the pickup signal is boosted by a pre-amp it can be plugged into the line input of a desk, but this is found only on the more expensive instruments. Some of the better models like Takamine and Washburn also have a basic

EQ section which can be quite useful. On pickups with no pre-amp a DI box or external pre-amp is usually necessary to match signal levels.

Mic and DI

You can use a combination sound of microphone and DI and you may well want to compare them for a given recording situation so it's always wise to try both side by side if a DI signal is available. The DI signal can often provide a percussive edge to the sound which adds attack and force to the miked up sound.

Watch out for phase problems if you decide to use both together. Some microphone repositioning may be necessary to get the signals in phase. You can also try using the phase reversal switch on the desk, if it is equipped with one.

Using effects

The acoustic guitar can sound great when used with effects – especially modulation like chorus and flange. Here the DI signal from a guitar pickup is a big advantage. It also gives the guitarist more freedom of movement with no mics to dictate the playing position.

Using a plectrum

Steel strung acoustics are often played using a plectrum and the plectrum thickness has a large influence on the sound. A light plectrum produces a sound with more presence and attack when strumming but requires a steady hand to give the best sound. If you are a heavy handed strummer belting out a political angst song, then the sound will be all attack and little note. And you'll probably rip the plectrum in half. A medium plectrum would be a better choice.

Obviously the material the plectrum is made out of also plays a part. Generally, harder material equals brighter. Some of you may remember brass plectrums or metal finger plectrums both of which have a distinctive metallic edge to the sound.

One thing that is useful in a recording session is a plectrum with some grip for the thumb and index finger. In the heat of the moment when that red light goes up for record you will probably need it to counter the effect of a nervous sweat!

Different tunings

Folk style acoustic guitar is often tuned differently. For example a 'D' modal tuning would be (from the low string up) D A D G A D. This gives the acoustic guitar a fuller sound with more low drone notes (many folk pieces are in the key of D) for accompanying songs and tunes. The method of miking remains the same but you will have to be more aware of potential boom on the bass end.

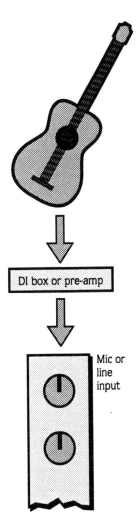

DI box or pre-amp

Mic or line input

Figure 4.6 Guitars fitted with pickups but no pre-amp will require an external pre-amp (with or without EQ) or a DI box to provide an adequate signal for a desk channel input

Capos

Many players prefer to use capos for compositions in different keys and there are good reasons for doing so. You can use open strings in your chord voicings more often and also take advantage of tunings like the D tuning mentioned above in other keys by strapping on the capo. For example with a capo on the second fret you would be in the key of E.

But how does this affect recording? It's only a problem when the capo is high up the neck because that takes all the bass out of the sound. After the fifth fret you will find this starts to happen. You can't find the bass from a capo'd guitar but you can add another guitar playing lower inversions without a capo as an overdub. Capo'd guitar can give really nice, bright sounding effects – sometimes even a little like mandolin, especially on the higher parts of the fretboard.

5

Miking electric guitars

It's just a question of shoving a microphone in front of a speaker isn't it? Well, yes, you can get a result that might work but there's a lot more involved if you want to get a first class sound. It's like the difference between thinking you know how a guitar lick goes and actually being able to play it. If you really know the lick, you've got the right notes under your fingertips and you can concentrate on the expression and the sound rather than fumbling around trying to remember how it goes. Miking the guitar is the same. If you know the mechanics of how to go about it you can concentrate on the fine detail – getting the best sound possible and making it work with the song – not worrying about where to position the mic or how to connect it to the console. Bearing that in mind, some knowledge of microphones, mic positioning and room acoustics is essential.

The Shure SM57, a well regarded dynamic mic

Playing set up

When playing live in the studio with a band you will probably have only one close mike on the speakers, unless you are using a stereo set up, whereas, in an overdub situation, you will be able to use a variety of microphones at different distances from the cab, if those extra mics are available.

Types of microphone

Dynamic microphones
This is the most commonly used microphone for close miking a guitar speaker. Luckily it's also one of the cheapest of the microphones I'm suggesting in this chapter, coming in at under a hundred pounds for a good quality model like the Shure SM57. Here are some more plus points for the dynamic microphone:

- Robust – I don't recommend dropping it on the floor to test it out, but yeah, it can take a few knocks and survive.

- High SPL – SPL? That's short for sound pressure level and I think
  we all know that high SPL means *loud!* For the rock sound you
  have to make those speakers work hard and not only can a
  dynamic microphone take this sort of punishment at close range,
  but because of the way it works a proportionately high level signal
  to the desk is the result.

Frequency characteristics

Treble – dynamics can't reproduce that really high presence because of
the way they're constructed. Yet, as most speaker cabs can't either (rarely
giving you anything above 3 kHz unless they're horn loaded) speaker and
mic are a good match. Most dynamics incidentally start losing their ability
to reproduce high frequencies around 12 kHz and up.

Bass – a useful thing for getting a beefy sound is actually a side effect of
the unidirectional microphone design. This is an increase in bass as the
microphone is placed closer to the sound source (the speaker in this case)
and is known as the bass proximity effect.

 As usual, there are some drawbacks:

- Low SPL – the microphone will put out a pretty poor signal level
  for quiet sounds like acoustic guitar and low level jazz guitar. This
  lack of signal can cause noise and level problems further along the
  signal chain for desk and multitrack recorder.
- Treble – because of its lack of presence, the dynamic will not
  reproduce the sparkling treble of an acoustic guitar or the modern
  zing of some clean electric sounds.
- Polarity – the pick up pattern of a dynamic is nearly always
  unidirectional. That is, from one direction only. This makes them
  better for multimiking. By pointing them at the target sound
  (speaker) other, unwanted sounds are picked up less.

Electret mics, like this AKG C1000 need to be powered either by a battery or from the desk (phantom power)

Condenser/electrets

We're getting into expensive territory here unless you should chance on a
secondhand bargain. What makes these microphones cost more is their
design and construction which involves expensive components including
some pre-amplification. So what do you get for the money?

- Frequency characteristics – This is an area where good
  microphones excel because they can reproduce faithfully the tonal
  qualities of the instrument, from bass all the way up to sparkling
  treble. Basically you get a truer sound.
- SPL – The more modern microphones can deal with loud rock
  stacks as well as low level acoustic instruments and mellow jazz.

But watch out for older designs and pencil shaped condensers which can be overloaded and damaged at high signal levels. Check with the dealer or read your microphone manual. If you need some sort of guide, a Marshall stack when cranked up loud could easily be delivering way over 100 dB SPL to the poor microphone close miking it!

- Polarity – The better models can pick up sound from all directions (omni pattern), not just in front of the mic. This makes them useful for getting that exciting and more natural live room guitar and amp mix. An omni pattern will also give a more natural sound, with less frequency side effects than a unidirectional microphone.

On the down side:

Handle with care! – Easily damaged, these are microphones you replace lovingly in their boxes after use and never drop. Avoid cheap electrets, which will have a sound to match the price.

Phantom powering

In condenser and electret microphones the movement of the diaphragm in the mic is small and the resulting electrical signal needs to be amplified. This amplifier in the microphone needs power from somewhere and in electrets this is provided by batteries, although some (such as the AKG C1000), can be powered from the desk like condenser mics by a +48 V phantom power supply. Most desks now have this built in but it's worth checking out before you buy the mic! No extra connections are needed because the desk sends power to the mic by cleverly using the microphone lead without interfering in the AC voltage signal from the mic itself.

PZM

These boundary effect microphones have been made popular by the cheap but useful Tandy model. PZM stands for Pressure Zone Microphone which is a pretty good description of where the mic works best too. The 'pressure zone' being created by sound waves hitting a fixed surface like a wall, floor or ceiling and creating a change in air pressure. This strong signal is picked up by a microphone – more often than not mounted on a small metal plate which both reflects sound to the microphone and picks up direct sound. It's not that successful for close miking the guitar but can be useful as a room microphone, or part of a stereo pair. There are other advantages:

- Cost – The Tandy PZM is extremely good value for money.
- Frequency characteristics – for a fraction of the cost you have a microphone that will reproduce the high frequency sounds.

- In the room – a cheap alternative to a condenser as a live room mic.

Disadvantages

- Output – fairly low but can be converted to phantom powering or, alternatively, connected to a balanced microphone input by changing the plug from a jack to XLR. This will give a higher level of signal to the desk.
- Tonal – needs to be mounted on a fixed surface to reproduce bass well. High frequencies can be a little on the thin side.

Sound direction (polar patterns)

Polar patterns show the pickup patterns of the microphone type

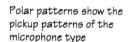

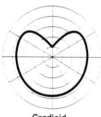

Cardioid

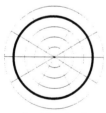

Omnidirectional

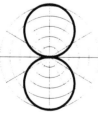

Figure of eight

I mentioned that some mics pick up sound from in front and others from all around. This is what is called a microphone *polar* pattern. Dynamic microphones nearly always pick up sound from one direction only – in front, and are called *unidirectional*. Electrets and condensers can vary, some even have switches to change between directional patterns.

Surely you only need to pick up sound from one direction?

Well not if you want to pick up the sound waves bouncing round a room or if you want a more natural sound. After all, with our ears we can hear from behind and to the side as well as from the front. On a microphone this would be called omnidirectional. Variations in pick up pattern are also found but these are the two most useful.

Choosing a pick up pattern

Unidirectional (also called cardioid) and hyperdirectional mics are used for close miking in a situation where you don't want spill from other instruments in the room.

Omnidirectional and *figure of eight mics* are used for close miking and where you want to pick up the sound of the guitar in a room and use the room reverberation characteristics. An omni pattern will give a more natural sound with a better bass response.

Equipment

Whatever style of music you play, rock, country and western, jazz or pop, the type of amplifier, cabinet and speaker size all have a part to contribute to the sound when miking up. The methods of miking the cab can, for the most part, be applied to any size of speaker whether it's a 5 inch or a 4 x12.

Humbuckers or single coil?
Lead or rhythm pickup?

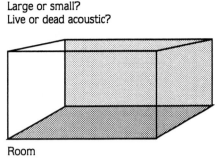

Large or small?
Live or dead acoustic?

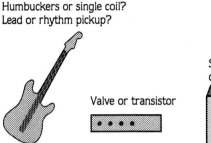

Speaker type and
cabinet size

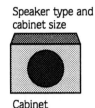

Valve or transistor

Guitar   Amp   Cabinet   Room

Figure 5.1 Some of the things
that influence the recorded
sound of the guitar

Speakers and cabinets

Most cabs use 10 or 12 inch speakers singly or in multiples, although it's
not unknown to mic up tiny practice amps with smaller speakers to get
that definitive sound! Open backed cabinets are usually found in combos
and can give a fatter sound than closed back cabs. It is also true that the
closed cab will have more noticeable resonant spots in the frequency
range caused by its dimensions.

Amps and speakers

Amplifiers will have an impedance rating clearly marked next to the
speaker output socket(s). Valve amp impedances are normally 8 or 16
ohms, and it is important that the speakers match the requirements of
the amp. I've already mentioned that valve amps can be damaged if they
are powered up without a speaker load.

Transistor amps are more robust and will state a minimum speaker
requirement. Speakers with a higher impedance will give a reduced output
level and less distortion, and vice versa for speakers with a lower
impedance. Beware of using cabs with too low an impedance if you want
your amp to last!

Amp and stack size

Big amp and speaker set ups are really effective only where the recording
studio area is big enough, not only to accommodate the rig, but to capture the monster nature of the sound using ambient microphones together with close ones. Remember that one microphone close miking a stack
of four by twelves is not likely to sound any different to one close mike
on a Marshall 50 and 2 x12. After all – you can only mic up one of the
speakers closely.

Speaker overdrive

When they're pushed, some speakers have cones which are designed to
add distortion at high power levels. Indeed expensive speakers can sometimes be accused of sounding too clean and clinical next to their poorer
brethren! For this reason the old Celestion range always sounded good
for rock guitar, and speakers like Electrovoice (which are far more efficient) work well for classy clean guitar.

No tweeters?

The sort of overdrive which dedicated guitar amp heads produce benefits from the high frequency filtering effect of speakers. The harsh, rasping tones are lost and the punchy mids and bass emphasised so using a full range speaker system including high frequency tweeters would in most circumstances simply add something you don't need.

Which speaker?

In a 1x12 combo you have no choice which speaker to mic up, but what if you have a cab with more speakers? With only one mic and a little time it's worth experimenting to see which one sounds best.

Close miking

For all close miking you can use a dynamic or a condenser capable of taking the high SPL produced at such close proximity to a speaker. You can put the microphone wherever you want if you get the sound you want – there are no hard and fast rules. Nevertheless a good starting point is pointing at the centre of the cone from the front of the speaker.

Front of speaker

The mic distance could be a few inches away from the speaker grill, pointing at the centre of the cone. Many engineers, myself included, prefer to put the microphone right up to the grill so that it's almost touching. This gives a more gutsy sound and takes full advantage of the bass proximity effect on the microphone. It also maximises the treble if the speaker points at the centre of the cone.

If this produces too brittle a sound try moving the microphone off centre, which has the effect of turning the treble down. In effect, you are using your microphone as a tone control by putting it into this off axis position.

Rear

Speakers can also be close miked from behind or to the side of the cab to achieve a sound. Even if they're in an enclosed cab some sound will still come from the sides and back, although the clarity and definition will be weakened.

Miking an open backed combo from behind will give you a mega bass response which can be very useful for sound layering or when you want a weighty, dark sound. Simply point the microphone at the back of the combo from a short distance away.

Little cab – big sound

Let's face it, small speakers rarely sound brilliant do they? Yet I've got a tale to tell here. Once I was recording a session and playing guitar in a large studio with a band. Half way through, my amp packed up. The only thing available was a little 10 watt practice combo. We managed to get a good sound out of it by putting it in a corner. Due to something called the 'boundary effect', which has the acoustical result of doubling the amount

INFO

You might think that because all the speakers are the same size and make that they'll sound identical but you'd be wrong. Wear and tear and different tolerances can mean that some speakers react differently to others – I've even recorded guitarists who haven't realised that some of the speakers in a cab are blown!

of bass, we were able to make the cab sound bigger. Miking it up from the rear also helped. The corner had to be fairly dry acoustically to avoid phase and comb filtering effects from sound reflections, but when we cranked the thing up it was session on!

Front and back

It's most often the case with combos that you love the bass response from the back of the cab but still want some of the clarity that the front miked position gave.

The answer is to use two microphones. One on the front and one on the back. These don't have to be the same make of microphone, you could even be using a condenser on the front and a dynamic on the back. Whichever method you use be aware of phase problems between the two microphones.

Remember that as the speaker is moving towards the front microphone it is moving away from the back one and vice versa – a perfect example of phase cancellation. Tonally you could lose some of that lovely bass or produce a sound which lacks clarity.

To get rid of this effect, try phase reversing the mic input channel on the back mic, or moving the mics until the effect is lessened. Yet the extreme tonal change may also be desirable and you should experiment with the fader levels of each mic channel on the desk, they don't have to be equal! In reality you're now using the phase as a tone control.

What is phase?

Most guitarists have tried out the phase effect pedal. A simple guitar phase pedal works by mixing a slightly delayed version of the signal with the original guitar sound. This gives the characteristic tonal colouration which can then be modified by modulation.

You get a similar tonal effect, minus the modulation, by using two microphones placed at different distances from a guitar speaker. The crucial factor is the delay, because sound waves coming from the speaker will reach one microphone fractionally ahead of the other.

When a big, thrangy chord is played the sound waves produced will travel at the speed of sound and reach the microphones at different times in their wave cycle. When those signals are summed together at the desk interesting things begin to happen. Some of the frequencies will be emphasised (in phase) and some cut (cancelled), depending on their time/wave cycle relationship when they hit the microphones. In sound terms this can affect the tone in a beneficial or bad way depending on the sound you are trying to achieve.

For example, one obvious side effect of extreme phase is a loss of bass, another is a loss of clarity in the mid frequencies.

Positively, if you have time to experiment with microphone positions you can start to alter tone with different mic positions.

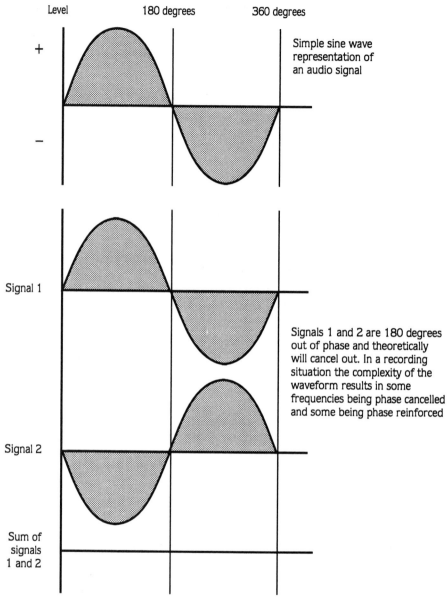

Level   180 degrees   360 degrees

Simple sine wave representation of an audio signal

Signal 1

Signals 1 and 2 are 180 degrees out of phase and theoretically will cancel out. In a recording situation the complexity of the waveform results in some frequencies being phase cancelled and some being phase reinforced

Signal 2

Sum of signals 1 and 2

Figure 5.2 Phase is measured in degrees. A complete wave cycle is 360 degrees.

Stereo miking and phase

If you want to use two microphones with no phase problem, they should be placed at the same distance from the sound source. However they do not have to be side by side – they could be spaced apart.

Console phase reversal switch

Tonal phase effects can also be achieved if you have a reverse phase button on the mixing console. This actually changes the waveform by 180 degrees, thus reversing its negative and positive positions.

Amp and cab

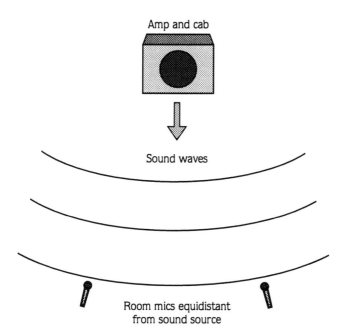

Sound waves

Room mics equidistant
from sound source

Figure 5.3 Ambient stereo
miking avoiding phase
cancellation. Both mics
should be at the same
distance from the cabinet.

Desk phase reversal can cure a phase problem between two mics, or mic and DI combinations, but eventually you may just have to get off the seat and change the microphone position!

Speaker phase

Incidentally, if you buy a secondhand cab that's had replacement speakers fitted, it's worth checking if they've been wired up correctly and not in anti-phase (with the positive and negative connections going to opposite terminals on one or more speakers). While some phase difference is acceptable, anti phase most definitely is not! This will cut a lot of bass out of the signal and result in a very weak sound.

Why doesn't the sound from the cab sound the same over the studio monitors?

This is a question that guitarists nearly always ask and it's especially noticeable when you're using overdrive sounds. Two factors come into play: mic position and room acoustics.

Mic position

One thing you may notice is that on a close miked amp the overdrive mix always seems heavier than the one you set up. This is because when you set up your sound you don't have your head as close to the speaker as the mic is – and neither would you want it to be! You're actually listening to the sound coming from your amp plus the sound of the amp in the room.

One solution to the problem is to put the microphone where you were originally stood to evaluate and set up your guitar sound. This could mean swapping the dynamic microphone for the accuracy and greater sensitivity of a condenser in an omni pick up pattern, as the signal level from a dynamic will lose strength. However, you could be creating problems for yourself by losing what you liked about the close miked sound – a full bass end and top end presence.

Here there are two possible solutions. One is to back off the overdrive on the amp and check the sound over the studio monitors until it is right. The second is to use two microphones – a remedy that is only possible if this is a guitar overdub, remember the problem of spill?

In my experience, the amount of distortion that you can get away with live, or in rehearsal for chordal work, is almost always too much and has to be reduced for recording.

Room acoustic
Thankfully the method of recording guitars in dry, acoustically dead booths is not as common as it once was and engineers are happier to experiment, especially for overdubs. To go from the live ambience and excitement of gigging to a completely dead studio sound surely puts the dampers on anyone unless a seventies sound is required. Even then, most good studio engineers understood the benefit of a live acoustic area – even if it meant using the stairwell outside the studio.

Rattle and buzz
Loose fittings like screws, speaker handles and speaker bolts can intro-duce an unwanted rattle into the guitar sound. Worse still are loose or torn speaker grills which make a buzzing noise as the force of the speaker causes them to resonate! Believe me, you can hear them, even when the guitar is loud, because the microphone is so close in to the cab. Remove the grill or gaffa tape the loose bit down and tighten up any fittings that rattle.

Room mics
When you're miking up a large cab like a 4 x12 you would normally close mic one of the speakers in the cabinet (after experimenting to see which one sounds best of course) and use one or more microphones in the room. This really means that you need the space to take advantage of the large sound that such a cab (or wall of cabs) throws out. Having a micro-phone in the room will also allow you to take advantage of the tonal colouration that the slight differences in the speakers produce to give you that big cab sound.

The type of microphone you will need is a condenser, electret or boundary effect microphone like a PZM. If you can use a more open polarity like a figure of eight or omni response on the room mic you can take full advantage of the room reverberation.

Room reverberation
This happens as the sound waves produced by the speakers hit the walls, floor and ceiling of the room and bounce off. The reflection pattern

becomes more complex as the sound wave having hit one surface at an angle then bounces into another and so on, rather like a squash ball in a squash court. The sound that the listener hears is the combination of the direct sound from the speaker and a delayed version from the sound reflections. These sound reflections happen so fast that you don't hear them as separate echoes but as one which lasts for a while then dies down – reverberation. The bigger the room the longer the reverb lasts because the sound reflections take longer to get to your ears.

The tone of the reverberated sound is also affected by the type of surface that the sound waves hit. You may have noticed that studio live rooms have hard surfaces like wood, stone and slate. these give a bright reverberation, whereas a heavily furnished room gives a dull and shorter reverb sound. Experiment by clapping your hands once in an empty room and listening to the sound die away, then do the same in a heavily furnished or carpeted room.

Create a live studio acoustic

If you take a DIY approach you can create a more reverberant acoustic in a room by using plywood, corrugated sheets, mirrors and even lino. Likewise you can damp down a room that is too bright with curtains, sleeping bags and duvets. However for a big cab the problem remains that you need a decent size room to get the full effect, bearing in mind that the lowest sound wave produced from the guitar could be around 13 feet long.

Positioning the room mic

The further away you get from the actual speaker the more you will hear the sound of the guitar in the room. If you have only one microphone try setting it up at different distances and recording the result. This trial and error method will help you be more objective about the sound on playback.

Directional mic

If you've only got a unidirectional microphone you don't actually need to point it at the cab, it could be pointed for example at a mirror on the back wall. This will give a brighter sound as the mirror surface reflects high frequencies well, but it will also increase the reverb against dry time mix as the sound takes a little longer to reach the microphone.

Omnidirectional mic

My personal favourite, a condenser microphone with this pick up pattern can be placed about 12 feet away from the cab at a height of about 6 feet off the ground to get the maximum effect of a live room. Never be afraid to experiment with the location of this microphone, or the room acoustic itself. Think of both as extra tone controls. Sometimes the sound can be interesting if miked from outside the room itself!

Multi-miking

In an overdub situation if the microphones are available it's common practice to try up to four microphones at once. The intention is not to combine them all, although if that sounds good – fine! Actually, you should
listen to them all individually, then try different combinations to see what
works best for different parts. Here's a suggested method:

mic 1	front of speaker, close to grill
mic 2	rear of speaker
mic 3	front of speaker, about 3 feet away
mic 4	room mic for ambience

Personally I would use dynamics (from among those suggested towards
the end of the chapter) for all except the room mic, which should be a
condenser or electret. Even so, the dynamics can be substituted by condensers or electrets, should a plethora of such expensive mics be available!!

Figure 5.4 A typical multi-mic
situation showing distance,
types of mic, and their pick
up patterns.

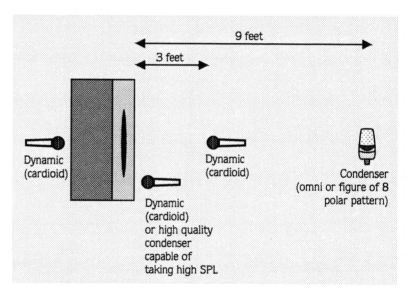

Recording the sound

If you're using more than one microphone, all the mics would be brought
up on separate channels on the desk but it would be a waste to record
them all to separate tracks. Instead they are usually sub mixed to one,
possibly two tracks if you want to keep the room mic separate.
Remember that when you submix the mics together the balance between
them cannot be altered once they've been recorded so it is important to
get the right balance – particularly between the ambient and dry mic.

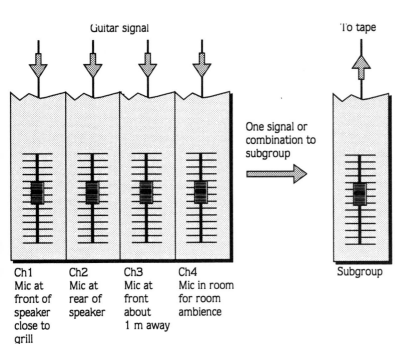

Ch1
Mic at
front of
speaker
close to
grill

Ch2
Mic at
rear of
speaker

Ch3
Mic at
front
about
1 m away

Ch4
Mic in room
for room
ambience

Subgroup

Figure 5.5 Pro studios often
use more than one mic on a
cabinet and choose the best
sounding combination to
send to tape

Stereo cabinets

The newer range of pre-amp/stereo power amp/stereo speaker set ups
mean that the guitar plus effects can be recorded in stereo if required.
The Marshall 1960A 4 x12's for example, have stereo speakers in one
cab, which rather defeats the object of wide stereo sound, but I suspect
it's probably done so that you only need take one out for a gig.

Live, the stereo effect of a single cab is going to be weak given the distance that the speakers are apart, but in the studio they can be close miked
with enough separation to create an impact when panned in the mix.

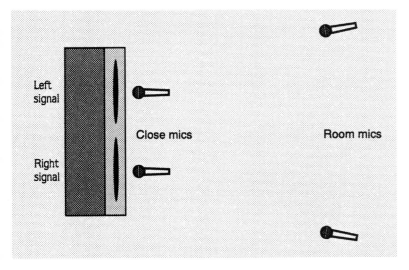

Figure 5.6A Stereo miking a
stereo cabinet

For most recorded guitar parts it's questionable whether you need to record with a stereo effect unless the sound is to feature heavily in a mix, or it really influences the way you play. Most home studio owners will not have the luxury of track space available anyway.

Microphones in guitars

Frank Zappa had a microphone built into the neck of his guitar and sometimes used this, or a mix of this and the standard pickup, to achieve the guitar sound. The different resonances picked up at this point give an altogether different tone as well as more fretting noise than the standard pickup position. Other electric guitars like the Shadow use this type of pickup to produce a pseudo acoustic guitar sound which is partially successful.

Miking up the guitar itself!

Believe it or not this works really well for certain tonal effects, especially with funk guitar. The idea is to capture the percussive and tight nature of the sound when the guitar is not amplified. For this reason, guitars with a maple fretboard seem to work best because of their harder sound.

Figure 5.6B Stereo miking two more cabinets. This will provide a more interesting sound with more separation between left and right. If the room mics are used, this should also give more width to the stereo sound and a more varied room interaction

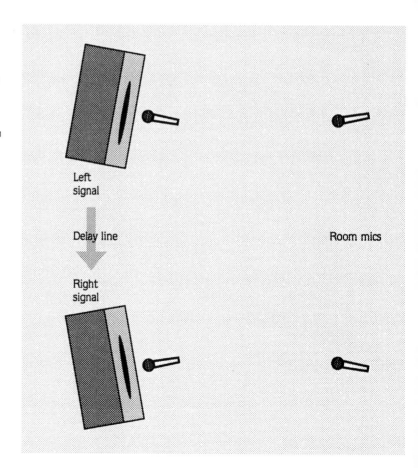

Left
signal

Delay line

Right
signal

Room mics

The microphone should be close in on the guitar, and preferably close to the fretboard, because the electric guitar unamplified is pretty quiet! You can record the part as an overdub, simply doubling up on what's already been played, or take the miked up amp sound and miked up guitar at the same time. The latter will work only if the guitarist plays in the control room and is connected to amp and cab in the studio area via a tie line. In this way the level of spill from the amplified guitar can be played at a controlled level over the studio monitors!

Suggested microphones

These are some of my tried and tested favourites, but the choice is a very personal thing and this list should not be taken as Gospel.

For close miking with Dynamics try the Shure SM57 and Sennheiser 441. The Sennheiser 421 is quite good for the rear of a cab and from a short distance away.

Condensers and electrets are more suitable for jazz or a more American rock sound when close miked – a little thinner with more edge. The following mics are also good for ambient miking: AKG 414, Neumann U87. Cheaper alternatives are AKG C3000 or 1000, Tandy PZM.

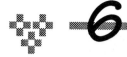

Guitar DI and speaker simulators

DI stands for direct inject. It's a way of recording guitar by taking the sound as directly from the source as possible – from the output of the guitar to the input of the desk for instance. Yet because a guitar amplifier can play such an important part in the sound too, many amps now provide a DI output. This allows you to use the tonal characteristics of the amp head for your recorded sound. Other methods include using DI boxes, speaker simulators or pre-amps – so which do you choose and when?

Guitar output – desk channel

For electric guitars and acoustics fitted with pickups this seems the simplest option. Just take the guitar lead, plug it into the guitar at one end and the desk line input at the other. It appears easy enough but unfortunately nothing is that simple. The problem is in the form of an impedance mismatch between the electrical output of the guitar and the desk input. Two things show this mismatch.

> 1 The guitar level is not very high on the desk input and you have to turn the desk input level up a lot to compensate. This reduces your signal/noise ratio.
> 2 The guitar sound is not as bright as it should be. You may then turn the desk HF EQ up to correct this and increase the level of hiss at the same time.

The DI box

A convertor called a DI box is the solution. This changes the high impedance output of the guitar to a low impedance signal which matches the desk. It allows an efficient signal flow, it may also increase the signal level and provide a choice of balanced and unbalanced outputs.

The DI box can be passive, battery or phantom powered and may offer a number of options:

DI box inputs

Instrument	A simple 1/4 inch jack connection from the guitar.
Microphone	Designed for mics, not guitars, this input may nevertheless be useful if your guitar has a particularly weedy output level.
Speaker	From an amplifier head speaker output, allowing you to use the amp head tone. Use a speaker lead, not an ordinary guitar lead to make this connection.

BEWARE! Do not plug a speaker output into an ordinary DI box input or desk line input. The speaker output from an amp is high level and will damage inputs that are not designed to take such a high voltage – probably with an accompanying puff of smoke!

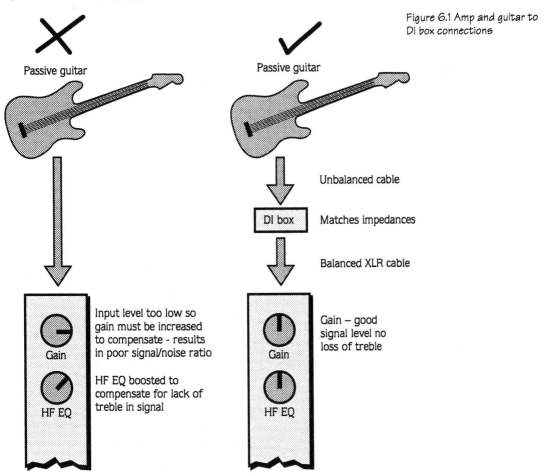

Figure 6.1 Amp and guitar to DI box connections

Sound manipulation

The more expensive DI boxes offer more to control the sound, usually in the form of switches on the box.

Attenuation	This allows you to alter the output level from the DI box by preset amounts, nominally between -20 and 0dB. Some desk inputs are easily overloaded and you may find this useful when you present the DI box with a high level signal such as a speaker output. On an active (powered) DI box you could also use this feature in reverse to boost a weak signal.
Earth lift	If you find once all the connections are made that there is a constant low frequency earth hum this switch will almost certainly eliminate it. If not then check the earths on all the equipment in your guitar set up.
Phase reversal	You may find this useful if you are using a combination of mic and DI and getting phase problems when listening to the combined signal on the desk. Sometimes reversing the phase can cure, or lessen this problem.

DI outputs

Unbalanced
An unbalanced output is a 1/4 inch jack socket which can be connected to the line input of a desk. In some cases where there is no alternative it can be used to carry signal on to an amplifier input (see later).

Balanced
The balanced (XLR) output is chosen by most engineers because it gives more level, you can use a longer cable run, the lead does not pick up interference noise and you can phantom power the active circuitry of the DI box from the desk using the balanced cable.

Speaker
If you are using a mic plus DI signal, your amp head will use this through connection to link with a guitar cab.

Active pickups
Acoustic and electric guitars which are fitted with electronic pre-amps often put out enough signal to drive a line level desk input. You may not need a DI box for recording such guitars, especially if impedance matching is also a part of the pre-amp circuitry. A balanced connection in the form of a stereo jack or XLR indicates that the guitar is geared up for studio performance requirements.

Using the DI box

Guitar – DI – desk
The DI'd guitar is at its best for clean, bright sounds and will work well with compression and chorus effects. After distortion the sound will be

harsh and fizzy because there is no filtering effect by speakers to reduce the bandwidth. The effects themselves can be added from recording outboard or pedal effects can be used in line before the DI box. Pre-amp effects outputs will not require a DI box.

Use for acoustic instrument pickups, clean electric guitar picking, chords, funk, skank, abrasive overdrive.

Guitar – amp – DI
You can DI from the amp in a number of ways.

Amp head DI
Via the amp head's own DI output if it has one – which may use unbalanced jack or balanced XLR connections. In addition, the best amplifier DI outputs sport their own independent volume control. Without this the DI output level is reliant on the front panel volume controls and these can easily be so high as to overload a desk input on the receiving end of the DI output!

Amp speaker output to DI box
Alternatively, you can use the speaker output into a DI box that will accommodate such signals. In common with an amp's own DI you will lose the filtering effect of the speakers and the sound will be brighter. The tonal qualities of your amp, valve or otherwise will still shine through.

Figure 6.2 Amp head DI using DI box or speaker simulator

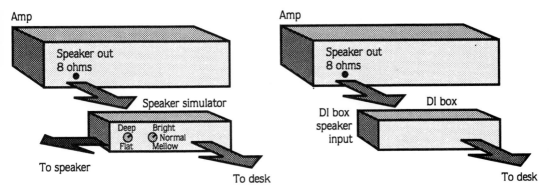

Use both the above methods for: Jazz, clean rock guitar, retro funk, country rock, brain shredding overdrive.

Caution! Unless otherwise stated in the manual, valve amplifiers need a speaker output load to function properly. Without such a load they will eventually break down, so do not disconnect the speakers when DI'ing an amp head unless you are sure no damage will result.

Speaker simulators
A dedicated speaker simulator unit will avoid the above problem by providing a dummy load for the speaker output in the form of a power soak. Combined with this will be a DI output, balanced or unbalanced and a

choice of EQ presets designed to simulate the most popular guitar speaker set ups. At the flick of a switch you could have a sound resembling a Marshall stack, Fender Twin, or jazz combo.

One big advantage the speaker simulation method of DI'ing has over a DI box is that the sound is more natural – incorporating the filtering aspects of real speakers. Another is that you can disconnect the speakers. This means that you can crank the amp up and drive it hard without annoying the neighbours. For some rock sounds this is essential and makes the Simulator a perfect tool for the small and semi pro studio as well as for the professionals.

For stand alone units the main disadvantage of the Simulator is the cost. Even so, it may be worth it as the sound quality is very close to a miked up cab without anything like as much hassle. This means that you can use it for most guitar sounds you want to record, from heavy rock, clean or overdriven, through to jazz. Many manufacturers, realising the importance of the Simulator output, now include it as a matter of course on pre-amps and effects units.

Combined miking and DI

The combination of bright DI and warmer miked up guitar cab can some-times produce very interesting results. Try these methods:

DI box before the amp plus miked up amp

The amp sound may be tonally very different or even overdriven but the DI sound will be clean and bright. Try mixing it with heavy overdrive 8:2 ratio in favour of the amp sound to add brightness and edge to the sound.

A useful production trick if you have enough tracks is to record the DI sound to one track and the miked up sound to another. If you don't like the amped up sound you can ditch that and run the DI'd version through another amp on the mix and mic it up. This has the advantage of retaining the feel of the original pass without having to do a retake.

DI from amp head plus miked up amp

This time you will retain the rawness of the amp sound but can add some edginess to distortion or some brightness to clean sounds by summing the signals. If phasing is present, use it only if it improves the sound. If it doesn't, experiment with phase reversal and different mic positioning.

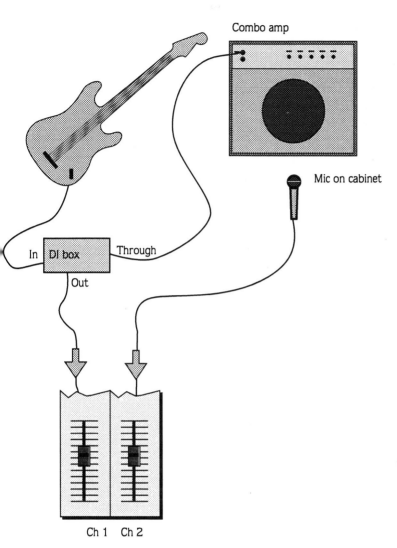

Combo amp

Figure 6.3 DI signal plus
guitar cabinet mic

Mic on cabinet

In DI box Through

Out

Ch 1 Ch 2

Amp vs DI chart

Miked up amp	DI
Filtering effect of speaker	Brighter sound
Natural speaker overdrive	Clean signal
Can use room acoustics	Using a simulator can create speaker characteristics and hard driven amp tones at lower, more controllable monitoring levels
Interaction between guitarist and amp	No room ambience and speaker to produce effects like feedback. A bit fizzy on distortion

7

Pre-amps

What is a pre-amp?

After the guitar electronics (which may be passive or active) the pre-amp is the first gain stage that the guitar signal meets. As far as electric guitars are concerned the design of the pre-amp these days is almost an amplifier in miniature, complete with overdrive, EQ and in the case of the more expensive versions, programmable effects. In this chapter we'll be looking at the pre-amp alone.

Design concept

The design concept is basically to copy the characteristics of a larger amplification set up without the problems of high volume levels or the hassles of carrying around a massive stack of gear! This makes it ideal for both home and professional recording. At home you can achieve those levels of overdrive and saturation without shaking the house and then having the neighbours round to shake you!

For the session guitarist some of the pre-amps are now so small that you can actually wear them as a matching accessory – OK if you've got to nip into the city centre studio and parking is restricted – you can get the tube or bus. Most pre-amps have headphone outputs too and some are both battery and mains powered so you can practice wherever and whenever you like.

Pre-amp vs. amp in the studio
Points for:

- Portable
- Convenient output direct to desk or amp set up
- Quick to set up
- Guitarist can play in the control room
- Good overdrive without high volume level
- Some are programmable
- Some have built in effects

Points against:

- No classic interaction between amp and speaker or tonal benefits of multi and ambient miking unless run through an amp and cab and miked up.
- High studio monitoring levels are required for controlled feedback effects.

The disadvantages of using a conventional set up can be overcome if you use both together. However this introduces another disadvantage – that of cost. You will need a power amp and cab, possibly even a stereo set up to make the most of the pre-amp. You also lose the advantage of portability.

Yet some pre-amps attempt to copy the effects of a miked up cab by using the speaker simulator outputs we've already discussed. We will be looking at that in more detail later but first let's look at the different types of pre-amp in more detail.

Does size really matter?

There are a confusing number of pre-amps to choose from and you have to pick what suits your needs and pocket (sometimes literally as well as figuratively!). Some are in the form of pedals, others as small as personal Walkmans; some are 1/3rd U size, some 1U rack mounting.

The budget versions generally have limited channel switching, outputs and effects, while the expensive ones are often MIDI controllable and programmable. Just like guitar amplifiers they have different tonal characteristics and it's worth trying out as many as you can until you find one that suits your taste and budget.

Floor vs. rack mounting in the studio

In the studio the idea is to have as little on the floor to trip over and break as possible. I've lost count of the number of jack leads and sockets that I've seen crushed underfoot, and equipment soaked in spilt coffee during recording sessions. Yet rack mounted gear is more expensive and less convenient to take out live unless you also invest in a flight case and a couple of pedal switches with long leads. Rack mounting pre-amps are therefore recommended for those musicians likely to remain in the studio, or able to afford a decent flight case and a guitar tech!

A mix of analogue and digital

Digital often seems to be a byword for 'better' in the recording world, but it is a dirty word as far as guitar pre-amps are concerned! No one has yet been able to come up with a decent digital overdrive – they all seem unnaturally clean and sterile.

Obviously the type of distortion guitarists like depends on the side effects of analogue technology as well as the mingling of circuit noise – eliminated from a digital device. In an expensive multi effects pre-amp combination, what you generally get is an analogue pre-amp with digital

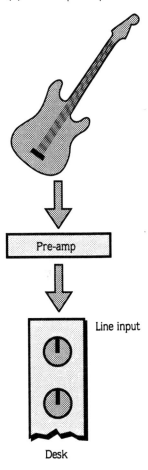

Figure 7.1 Using the pre-amp for recording
(a) Guitar – pre-amp – desk

Pre-amp

Line input

Desk

Figure 7.1 Using the pre-amp
for recording
(b) Guitar – pre-amp – amp –
speaker

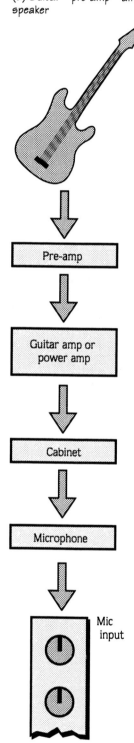

Pre-amp

Guitar amp or
power amp

Cabinet

Microphone

Mic
input

Desk

effects. Even so, some designers like Digitech and Alesis use analogue compression before passing the signal to digital reverb and delay sections.

Valve vs. solid state

Yes, that old chestnut! This, my friends is entirely down to taste …

Valves

I remember the old Watkins Copycat made a brilliant valve guitar pre-amp if you just ran the guitar into it and forgot about the echo part! Most dedicated valve pre-amps these days seem to favour the 12 AX7 (British ECC 83) valve and may have one or two inside the chassis. On a good unit like the Mesa V Twin they are quick and easy to change too. In common with their larger counterparts there are distinct tonal variations. For example the Marshall JMP 1 is excellent for harder rock sounds, whereas the Mesa V is fantastic for blues. However, given the amazing tonal variation available from modern EQ you can achieve almost any sound you want. As a rule valves are characterised by a warm, rounded tone for clean sounds and fat, saturated sustain for lead.

Most valve pre-amps sound excellent using the simulator output into the desk. If you want that extra presence on clean sounds try the direct output instead.

Solid state

Since the glory days of the Tom Scholtz Rockman, solid state pre-amps can claim to have come of age in units like the truly amazing Sans Amp PSA 1. This does a mighty fine job of recreating the tube amp circuit using solid state technology. It also uses EQ pre and post overdrive to allow a very wide range of sounds. Budget pre-amps can be a useful purchase but usually suffer from all the things guitarists despise about solid state – gritty rhythm overdrive and lack of warmth. Usually brighter, clean sounds are achieved with solid state but nothing yet has quite matched the clear, glassy tones of the Rockman. This was a firm favourite in the mid eighties and can be heard on loads of hit records from that era.

The sometimes thinner sound of solid state can make it easier to place sounds in a mix where there is a lot going on. To emulate the fatter valve style sounds you will have to use some creative EQ (see below), and for overdrive a simulator output is usually better. However for bright, clean guitar and edgy distortion try taking the simulator off.

EQ

If you want to create a lot of different sounds on the pre-amp then a good EQ section is essential. We've already talked about the filtering effects of the simulator output and how useful that can be in the studio, but this may be only a part of what's available. On a pre-amp with a lot of options it is the combination of all these tone shaping parameters that make the sound.

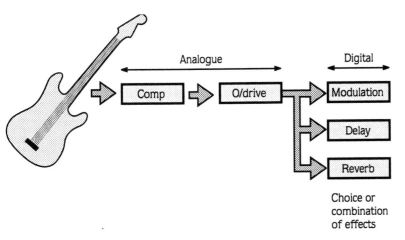

Figure 7.2 Analogue front end, digital FX

At one extreme you have a complicated unit like the Alesis Quadraverb GT. Here the EQ section offers almost too many options! In the EQ section you have parametric EQ, tunable resonators, and graphic EQ, while in the pre-amp you have bass and presence boost plus two kinds of cab simulation. You also have the option of running the EQ section pre or post pre-amp, and it's all programmable.

At the other end of the spectrum the Session Award JD10 offers passive three band EQ, that's LF, Mid and HF, but also has a speaker simulator option. This cuts the HF harmonics and boosts at 3 kHz for a little more bite.

> **TIP**
>
> *The simpler the pre-amp EQ the quicker you can set up the sound but your range of available sounds is more limited and you can't store them.*

Some classic pre-amp EQ settings for recording

Much of the sound is obviously dependent on the type of guitar you use but some EQ can give it that little bit extra. Treat the suggested settings as a starting point and edit to suit.

Jazz
A neutral sound is needed with no excessive EQ. To produce a rounded tone you may want to cut some treble at 6 kHz or so by a few dB's.

HF	Mid	LF	Simulator
–3 dB at 6 kHz	–	–	√ Small cab

Country
A sparkling clean sound needs some extra presence and some pre-amps are equipped with just such a control. If yours hasn't got one try using the HF.

HF	Mid	LF	Simulator
+6 dB at 8 kHz	–	+3 dB at 250 Hz	optional

Skank

Reggae and ska rely on a thin, choppy sound. Using the simulator will give a more old fashioned amp tone, leaving it off will make it brighter, especially if you want to riff as well as play chords. The bass cut allows the treble attack and chop of the sound to come through.

HF	Mid	LF	Simulator
+6 dB at 8 kHz	–	–4 dB at 200 Hz	–

Funky Strat

Notice how the mid cut on this seems to bring out the treble and bass nicely. This is improved with some compression.

HF	Mid	LF	Simulator
Bright	–6 dB at 700 Hz	+3 dB at 150 Hz	√ Small cab

Classic Motown

At the Motown studios the actually guitar cab speaker was just used for monitoring purposes, and the amp became in effect a huge DI box. Of course valves had a big part to play then, so a valve pre-amp stage is going to get closer to the sound of the time.

HF	Mid	LF	Simulator
–	–6 dB at 700 Hz	–	–

Classic clean Rockman

The Rockman sound can be copied to some degree by using a large amount of boost at 6 kHz and loads of compression. Better still, use an enhancer to obtain the glassy tones and high harmonic content.

Rhythm overdrive

This should really allow the character of the guitar to come through. Most manuals that come with pre-amps will give suggested settings, and for blues and some pop rhythm you only need a hint of overdrive to give the sound bite. I'm working on a universal 0 – 10 scale of overdrive but once again, treat these suggested settings as a starting point.

Blues rhythm
Set overdrive to 4. You shouldn't really hear the overdrive until you dig in on the chords.

HF	Mid	LF		Simulator
–	+6 dB at 1kHz	+4 dB at 250 Hz		√

Melodic pop rhythm
Overdrive 4. Again the overdrive shouldn't be obvious until the guitar dynamic comes up. The whole point of the sound is that it has clarity, but is on the edge of being dangerous.

Leaving the simulator off adds a brightness which it is harder to get using the HF control. The lower mid range boost gives it the feel of a 2x12 combo, something like a Fender Twin. On some pre-amp EQ the LF range can be used to control the lower mids too.

HF	Mid	LF	Simulator
Bright	+4 dB at 250 Hz	–	–

Heavy rock rhythm
Overdrive – 8. To achieve the classic 'chunk' when vamping, some of the attack is brought out using the upper mid control. The LF boost gives the impression that the sound is coming from a bigger cab.

HF	Mid	LF	Simulator
–	+4 dB at 3 kHz	+3 dB at 100 Hz	√ large cab

Use the mix control
If your pre-amp has a mix control between it and the direct sound you can mix some direct sound back in to keep the guitar's tonal character. Try starting with a mix of 80% pre-amp.

You can also create the impression that you have DI'd the guitar at the same time as you pre-amped it by using a higher balance of direct sound in your mix. Say 60% pre-amp.

Some pre-amps like the Boogie Twin allow you to set up a mix between the dirty and clean channels which can achieve a similar effect.

Lead

When talking about pre-amp lead sounds, reviewers often mention the second harmonic creeping in over the note. Basically this second harmonic is an octave above the note you're playing. Yet many other squealing harmonics can be brought in using overdrive by the guitarist with a good technique. Changing plectrum position and dynamic, 'digging in', and using 'pinch harmonics'.

Another thing to look out for, especially with solid state pre-amps is the way the distortion falls off into a kind of fizz as the note dies away. Sometimes this is a non too subtle noise gate, but even without a gate it's fairly common and a lot of HF boost will only make it more noticeable.

British

The classic British sound requires some heavy EQ notching in the mid range. Resonant filters can be used if your pre-amp has them to recreate the well known phase and harmonic valve sound. This may already be built into your overdrive circuit for solid state pre-amps. Valve pre-amps should not need such heavy EQ. Set overdrive 8 – 10.

HF	Mid	LF	Simulator
+ 4 dB at 3 kHz	–6 dB at 640 Hz and 1.5 kHz	+6 dB at 100 and 250 Hz	√ Large

American

Overdrive 8 – 10. Generally speaking, the American sound tends to have more mid range resonance and less of the warmth. A graphic EQ can be useful here for more wide band effects. For more extreme settings use a true parametric EQ. Here selected harmonics can be emphasised using the boost control and a fairly tight Q.

Low output pickups

Sometimes guitars just don't seem to have that humbucking overdrive sound you want because the pickups don't sound fat enough or are weak. To compensate you can use a pedal overdrive in line with a pre-amp overdrive or anything that can act to boost the signal, like a compressor. This may bring up the level of noise but may well do the trick for lead playing.

Expanding the tonal range of the pre-amp in the studio

Before the pre-amp

There are many pedals on the market which will shape sound. The easiest to operate are graphic equalisers but a decent parametric will give you more specific control. Remember that this affects only the guitar tone before it goes into the pre-amp.

Pre-amp effects loop

Provided your pre-amp has an effects loop a better EQ could be patched in. This may be pre or post overdrive in the signal path, dependent on the pre-amp model.

Using the desk

Desk EQ is often better than basic pre-amp EQ, particularly in the critical mid range. You can also patch in EQ like a graphic or parametric to alter the post pre-amp sound.

Creating a speaker simulator style EQ

If your pre-amp doesn't have a simulator output try this EQ:

10 – 12 kHz HF	cut by – 6 dB
100 – 200 Hz	boost by + 3 dB

The lower the LF boost the bigger the size of the simulated cab. Or use a noise gate filter with the low pass filter set at 8 kHz and the HPF at 20 Hz. Add some bass using the desk EQ as above and some upper mid boost at 2-3 kHz for extra bite if required.

Resonant filters

We talked about different types of EQ earlier in the book but not reso- nant filters because they are not normally found on mixing consoles. The resonator is a sharp filter tuned to a very narrow frequency band – so sharp in fact that you can pick out notes with it. On a pre-amp equipped with it you can emphasise the fundamental frequencies and the harmonic overtones that make up the character of the guitar sound. It is particular- ly useful when trying to recreate the characteristic phase and harmonic overtones of valve amps.

Resonator chords

Some really interesting chordal effects can be obtained when you have two or more resonators and a long decay:

Resonator 1	Resonator 2	Resonator 3
C	E	G
Fundamental	+5 semitones	+7 semitones

However if the mix of harmonic to pre-amp is now high you can really only get the benefit when you're playing C, and other notes will sound pretty strange! It's often wise to stick to root, fifth and octave.

Programmability and overdubbing
It's very useful to go into the studio with your sounds already programmed up and ready to go, which expensive pre-amps like the Sans Amp PSA1 and Marshall JMP 1 allow. Yet it's by no means essential. Most recording using different guitar sounds is done as an overdub, using a separate track if one is available. This allows ample time to change sounds using the simple controls of a budget pre-amp like the Sessionmaster JD 10.

Which output?

Once you're plugged in and ready to go, a good pre-amp will offer you a wide choice of outputs. All are useful for recording:

Headphone output

Pros
Great for practising, especially in the studio with personal headphones on while you're waiting to do your take. But watch out – if the studio monitoring is quiet everyone will be able to hear a tinny sound escaping from your headphones and this is quite off-putting to the other musicians.

Cons
You can try the headphone output into the desk if you want but it's generally quite toppy, probably has an impedance mismatch and is not as good quality as the other outputs.

Direct output

Pros
This is the equivalent of an amplifier DI and will generally give you a good, bright clean sound.

Cons
The overdrive sound is likely to be fizzy and unnatural.

Comments

If you have no other outputs you can always equalise the signal with some high frequency cut on the pre-amp itself or use a desk EQ. Some guitar parts actually benefit from this toppy overdrive sound too, so don't discount it entirely.

Simulator output

Pros

Simulates the effect of using a speaker by filtering out treble harmonics above 6 kHz. Some add bite around 3 kHz. Overall a more natural sound suitable for jazz, blues and rock. It's better for the classic sounding overdrive too.

Cons

Not so good for modern funk, or bright sounding clean guitar.

Comments

Preset on smaller units and adjustable on more expensive ones, nearly all pre-amps now have some sort of simulator output. Designed to emulate set ups like Marshall Stacks and Fender Dual Showmans they normally incorporate some form of EQ filtering and sometimes phase shift.

Levels and connections

Budget units usually offer unbalanced mono or stereo jack outputs, and the more expensive units a choice of balanced or unbalanced jacks and XLR's respectively.

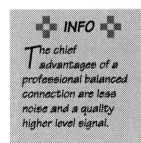

INFO

The chief advantages of a professional balanced connection are less noise and a quality higher level signal.

Unbalanced

Operate at around −10 dBV and can be connected to unbalanced desk line inputs and amplifier inputs via mono jacks.

Balanced

Operate at 0 to +4 dB. Connect to console balanced line inputs (stereo jack) or desk microphone input (XLR). Guitar amps are not usually equipped with balanced inputs, the level of which will easily overload the input stage. Power amps for guitars on the other hand, often have a choice of balanced or unbalanced connections.

Recording a pre-amp through an amplifier and cab

The amp itself could be a power amp or an amp head. Ideally a power amp causes less problems with level matching as it can operate at −10 or +4 dB. Nevertheless most pre-amps have a variable output, and you can avoid overloading the input of a guitar amp head or combo (which is expecting a lower level signal) by turning the pre-amp output down.

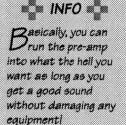

You can use the direct or the simulator output for this, and compensate for any unwanted changes to the sound with EQ. The direct sound may be a little bright and the simulator not quite bright enough.

And while we're on the subject of sound colouration there is a school of thought that says you must run a valve pre–amp into a valve power amp. If you are a purist, this option will appeal to you although you can get perfectly good results by using a solid state power amp. However, the logic of running a solid state pre-amp into a valve power amp has more going for it!

Once connected to the power amp/amp and speaker, let rip and check the sound out. You will probably want to modify the EQ a little – remember that 4 x 12's give more low bottom end and less clarity, while smaller speakers give a tighter bass response and a zingy upper mid. If you've already tried to simulate this in your pre-amp program you may just have to un-simulate it when you're plugged into the real thing! Once you've got the sound, mic it up in the manner described in the chapter on miking the guitar.

8

Using effects

The number of effects available to guitarists is truly mind boggling! Rows of gleaming and brightly coloured pedals fill the counters of guitar shops, racks of multieffects units and pre-amps with flashing LED's and high tech LCD's make the place seems more like the bridge of the Starship Enterprise! It seems that there is now an effect for every conceivable occasion, so how would you choose what to use in the studio, and perhaps more important – when to use it.

Pedal vs. rack effects

It seems that in some guitar magazines there is a backlash against rack effects. This is mainly to do with sound and ease of use. Yet rack effects have a lot of plus points for studio use.

Rack effects

Pros
Many effects in one unit
Portable
Switchable input and output levels
Programmable effect and signal path configurations – instant recall of favourite effects settings.
May include guitar pre-amp
MIDI and footswitch controllable
Can double up as studio multieffects unit.
No messy wiring

Rack effects

Cons

Can be complicated to program

Visually poor control – often only one parameter can be seen and adjusted at a time.

Real time adjustment of effects tricky without a MIDI pedalboard.

All effect types by the same manufacturer

Pedal effects

Pros

Easy to operate.

Visual cross referencing of effects settings useful.

Effects combinations using different manufacturers' pedals possible.

No understanding of MIDI necessary.

Old pedals often have more extreme and interesting settings.

Analogue and digital effects available.

Cons

Battery operated unless a power supply used.

Incompatibility of pedals and power supplies.

Lots of messy wiring.

Can be noisy.

Operating levels not suitable for studio line level equipment.

Non programmable

Some cons of both can be overcome. Your favourite pedal effect can be run on a rack multieffects send /return for example. And pedal effects levels can be brought up to studio line levels.

Pedal effects

Pedals, whether singly or arranged in pedalboard form, can be used to create some amazing guitar effects and sound textures. Often certain pedals become an integral part of a guitarist's sound – such as the Big Muff fuzz, Electro Harmonix Electric Mistress Flanger, MXR dynacomp or more recently the Rat overdrive and the Boss delay. Pedals such as these are designed to be used primarily in the live situation but will work equally well in the studio provided they are plugged into a guitar amp and miked up.

Signal level matching

Just plugging a pedal into a desk using the same method as for studio outboard produces a signal level matching problem between the pedal's −10 dB to −20 dB operating level and the desk's +4 dB. However there are ways to match signal levels.

Figure 8.1 Signal level matching effects pedals and desk inputs

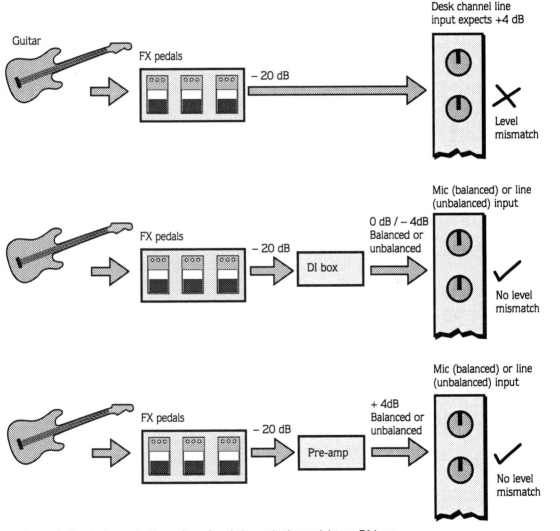

One solution is to route the guitar signal through the pedal to a DI box and then on to the desk. A disadvantage with this method is that you do not get the filtering effect of the speaker so the sound will be bright – but that can work to your benefit sometimes.

Another solution is to run the pedal effects through the pre-amp.

Desk effects and return

Pedals are sometimes used on desk effects sends, although it is not strictly the 'done thing'. Most desks operate at + 4 dB although portastudio effects loops may be −10 dB. On larger desks the send could overload the pedal and the return will not be enough to drive the desk input. Even so, as the send level from the desk is variable you can turn it down and so avoid overloading the pedal. This leaves us with the problem of the return level from the pedal to the desk. Any unit that can pre-amp incoming level could be used in line with the desk here − such as a compressor or even a DI box.

This is a lot easier with effects that have their levels matched.

Multieffects and signal levels

In the case of multieffects and combined pre-amp/effects units the −10 dB/ +4 dB switching gets round the problem of signal level matching.

Recording vs. mixing with effects

One of the questions I get asked most often is whether you should use effects when recording or add them at the mixing stage. While using overdrive and wah wah are obviously necessary when doing the take, the use of other effects is not so clear cut.

Recording with effects

Pros

Effects influence the way you play, especially echo.

Effects may be an important part of the guitar take character and tone.

Using them while recording frees them up for the mix.

Cons

Once recorded, effects cannot be separated from the dry sound and erased unless they are recorded to separate tracks.

Mix of dry and wet has to be right because you cannot change the balance later unless the effects are recorded to a separate track.

On small multitracks you do not have enough tracks to record effects to their own tracks.

Stereo effects can be created from dry mono guitar tracks on mixdown. This uses up fewer tracks than recording a mix of dry and stereo effect.

Some effects, particularly reverb are better left to the mix because the quality of studio digital reverbs is better.

Concerning this last point, some studio engineers attempt to bully guitarists into using the studio's more expensive effects but often they just don't sound the same or are too clean. It is true that pedal effects are noisier, but if you want to keep your own sound and avoid having the 'studio sound' of a particular studio, then stick to your guns. If a studio engineer tells you you simply can't use your own effects without good reason, then he's not the right one for you.

Mix wet and dry

One of the things that guitarists like to do is turn things up to max. and that goes for effects too. Yet turning your effects section balance to full effect and no dry signal is not going to make you sound like your favourite guitar hero.

In fact the effect mix for most sounds is 50% dry or more, with the obvious exception of distortion and pre-amp mixes. And having too much effect can ruin a sound. For example if all your mix is reverb, because this is a delay effect it will give the impression that you are playing at the bottom of a very large hole, or in another room down the hall from the rest of the band!

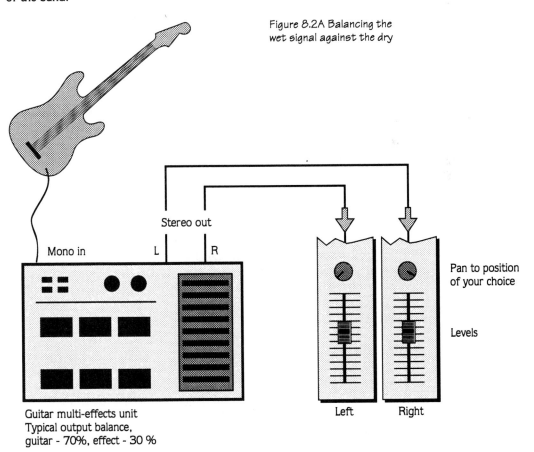

Figure 8.2A Balancing the wet signal against the dry

Figure 8.2B Using a
multieffects unit on desk
outboard.

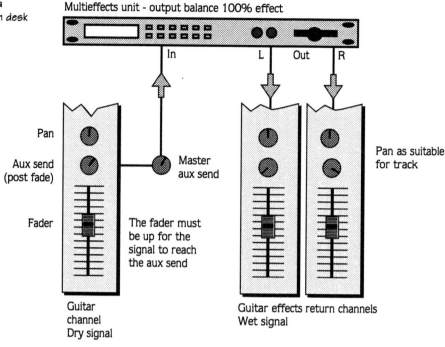

Compression in the studio

Why do guitarists need compression? One reason is that compression equals sustain and increased apparent volume. This is a creative use of the effect, but a studio engineer will also use compression to prevent overloading the level of the signal to tape. The trouble is that if the dynamic of a piece of music changes from quite quiet to RADICALLY LOUD some tape machines can't cope with it because they have a limited dynamic range. A bit like trying to squeeze a camel through the eye of a needle, so to speak.

A compressor can prevent overload because it works like an automatic amplifier volume control. When the level of your signal hits a preset level called a *threshold*, the compressor goes to work by turning the signal down by a preset amount – determined by a *ratio* control. You just set it up so that the loudest guitar signal simply cannot ever get high enough to overload the tape.

To tape
Usually the compressor is only needed for clean guitar where the dynamics are badly played. A threshold set to trigger gain reduction only on the peaks at a ratio between 2:1 and 5:1 should do the trick. Attack fairly fast – if you are losing the attack of the guitar itself then lengthen it on the compressor and check that your threshold is not set too low. Release should be set to fit the part being played. Start at a medium setting and adjust to suit.

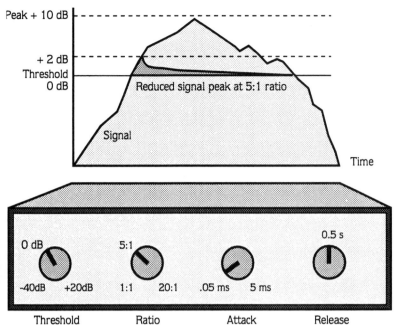

Figure 8.3 The compressor, and how it controls signal level to tape

Sustain

Pedal compressors or 'sustainers' are often used by guitarists, and compression is usually found in guitar multieffects units. Often the level of control is not as good as the studio version which can emulate all those sounds without losing as much of the high frequency.

Suggested settings

- Ratio   6:1 – 10:1
- Attack   medium
- Release long

Swell guitar

If you apply a lot of compression it will dip the level of the guitar attack and the compressor can then appear to increase the level as it returns the signal to unity gain with a long release. The drawback is the amount of noise but this can be carefully gated out using an expander gate of the type often found on rack mounting compressors.

Suggested settings

- Ratio   10:1
- Attack   fast
- Release long

Noise gates

Like compressors, noise gates are often found in guitar pre-amps. There is a good reason for this – pre-amp overdrive is a *noisy* business! You must have noticed that satisfying devilish hiss appear once you switch into overdrive – it's all part of the excitement of going a little bit over the top. However, in the studio this can prove to be a pain in the butt if it is audible in quiet sections, so a noise gate is used to get rid of the noise in the gaps between the played notes. If the guitar signal falls below the preset *threshold* level the gate closes and no signal is allowed through. This means that you have to set the gate threshold so that it is below the level of the quietest guitar part and above the level of the hiss.

Figure 8.4 The noise gate. Once the guitar signal is above the threshold, the gate will open. When it falls below it, the gate will shut. Attack, release and decay determine the finer points of the gate action with regard to time

Timing

The art of using the noise gate is to get it to close without cutting the start and end of notes or interfering with the tail end of the decay. Time parameters – attack, hold and decay – look after this, so it's better to use

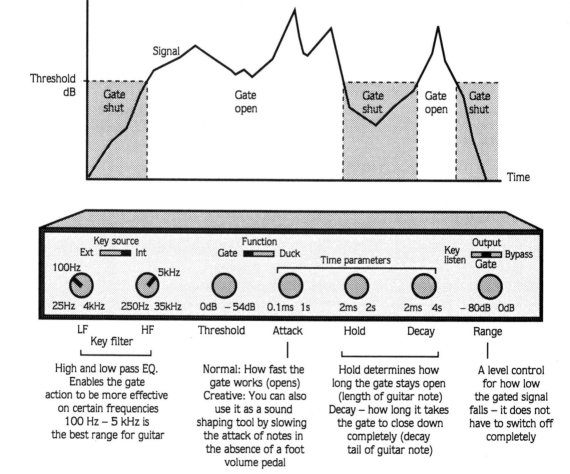

a good studio noise gate as opposed to a pedal that doesn't have these controls. Some of the gates found in more expensive pre-amps are up to the job and a good noise gate will have a quicker reaction time and an EQ section.

Of the two popular types of gate available, expander gates are better at tracking the dynamics of a guitar part than simple switching gates.

Gate filter

Most overdrive guitar signals do not contain much in the way of HF signal. A dynamic filter which drops the bandwidth as the volume drops could be a useful addition to the armoury against noise.

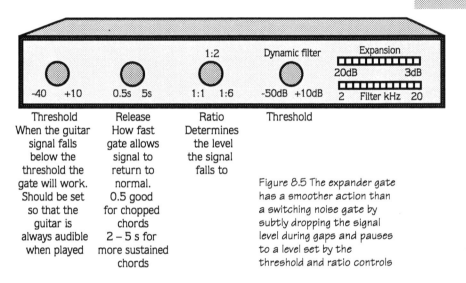

Threshold	Release	Ratio	Threshold
When the guitar signal falls below the threshold the gate will work. Should be set so that the guitar is always audible when played	How fast gate allows signal to return to normal. 0.5 good for chopped chords 2 – 5 s for more sustained chords	Determines the level the signal falls to	

Figure 8.5 The expander gate has a smoother action than a switching noise gate by subtly dropping the signal level during gaps and pauses to a level set by the threshold and ratio controls

Creative use of the gate

Most guitar players think that a noise gate is just used to cut noisy overdrive signals, but there are many other things you can do with a gate and a bit of ingenuity!

Triggering the gate

Once you've tried this you'll realise that you've heard it on lots of records.

1 Switch the gate into external key trigger mode.
2 Run an overdriven guitar signal into the noise gate input and send the key trigger input a rhythmic percussive signal. Try simple eights from the rhythm with a short decay time set on the gate.
3 Play a chord and you will hear it chopped into the same rhythm as the trigger.
4 Monitor loud and let the guitar go into feedback!

Figure 8.6 Triggering the
noise gate
A From guitar or pre-amp
direct to desk

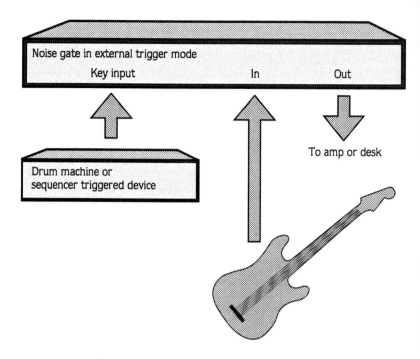

B From desk using direct or
off tape guitar signal

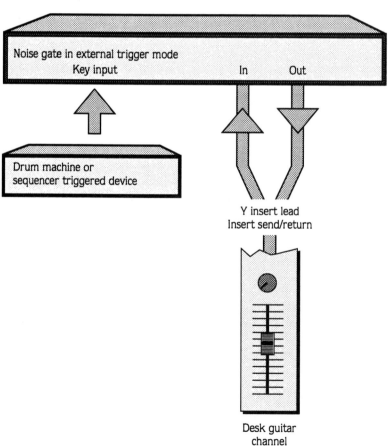

Sound shaping

Heavy gating with a slow attack time can alter the guitar attack to give impressive bowed in effects. Try playing single notes slowly on the lower strings for a cello-like sound. It will also work with overdrive switched in.

It is important to let the gate shut before you play the next note otherwise it will not retrigger the slow attack as the gate is already open.

Simulator EQ

If you are DI'ing the guitar or using a pre-amp with no simulator output you can use the gate filter EQ to cut any unwanted brightness out of the sound.

Tremolo

Tremolo is one of those effects that is just much better on amps and in pedals. The earthiness of the sound is completely lost by digital equipment. Try it with a middly sounding guitar and a touch of distortion for the classic sound.

Delay effects

It might surprise you to learn that effects like chorus, flange and phase are actually created using a short delay and some modulation. To set them up you need to hear the dry sound as well as the wet in the mix. This is so you can hear the modulated version working against it. Start with a 50:50 mix of dry and wet.

Width (depth) measures how far away from the original pitch the sound is taken; speed (rate) is how quickly the modulation occurs; feedback (regeneration) decides how much of the delayed signal is fed back into the signal. Phase is normally between 0.1 and 5 ms

Phase is underused by guitarists these days and probably remembered for retro funk rhythm and test card music. Yet Hendrix used phase successfully with overdrive and you can also use phase as a tone changer for the poor man's version of the big cab and valve sound.

Some sample settings

As usual with all the examples, treat them as a starting point and edit from there.

Retro funk

- Delay   3 s
- Speed   50 %
- Depth   50 %
- Feedback   positive 40 %

Valve phase

- Delay   2 ms
- Speed   slow (0.1Hz)
- Depth   40 %
- Feedback   positive 50 %

You can actually tune the harmonics of your phase by varying the delay and width controls. The more feedback you have the more extreme the effect of some frequencies being phase cancelled and others emphasised. In a way, using this method is better than having a fixed pitch resonator because it will alter harmonic as you change notes. The slow speed is crucial as a higher speed will cause a 'comb filter' sweep through the harmonic series of what you played.

'Vocal' phase

With a good delay unit you can actually pinch the frequencies quite hard and use the extreme characteristics of negative phase to bring out a vocal tone.

- Delay   1.5 s
- Speed   slow
- Depth   40 %
- Feedback   negative 100 %

Flange 5 – 12 ms

Flange is produced using a slightly longer delay time and is characterised by the lower frequencies of its sweep. Most incrementally programmed digital units produce a pretty weedy version of this effect, with none of the extremes that old fashioned pedals and rack units can achieve. Forget the noise and get hold of an Electro Harmonix Electric Mistress if you really want to go to town! Even a Boss analogue flange pedal can produce excellent results.

Classic flange

- Delay   11 ms
- Speed   slow (1 Hz)
- Depth   50 %
- Feedback   80 %

Eighth note vamping flange sweep
Adjusting the depth control on the above example to max. and vamping on eights brings out the pitch sweep well. If you choose your moment right on the recording you can create a pitch up or a pitch down sweep. Experiment with a longer delay too.

Chorus 8 – 25 ms
Chorus fares surprisingly well on digital effects units, even though it is in some ways a less extreme version of flanging. The delay time is longer and the effect more subtle but you have to be careful of taking the guitar out of tune at longer delay times with a wide width.

Classic chorus

- Delay   15ms
- Speed   30 %
- Depth   20 %
- Feedback 0

Extreme chorus
Can be very effective, especially when the guitar is taken to its limits with tuning – Banshees guitar fans look out!

- Delay   20 ms +
- Speed   45 %
- Depth   40 %
- Feedback 10 %

Classic Leslie guitar modulation
On an old delay unit this can sound great:

- Speed   Fast
- Depth   30 %
- Delay   15 ms +
- Feedback low

If you have a programmable effects unit you may be able to control the Leslie speed via MIDI controller messages for a more authentic sound.

Artificial double tracking (ADT) 25 – 80 ms
If you are short of tracks but want a double tracked effect on the mix try this as a starting point:

- Delay time   20 – 60 ms
- Feedback   single repeat
- Modulation   off, or try small depth and speed
- Pan   dry and wet signals hard left and right

Lead guitar ADT

ADT was also very fashionable in the mid eighties among lead guitarists and has a bit of an LA session man sound to it.

- Delay time   60 ms
- No modulation or feedback
- Mix   65 % dry

Slapback delay 80 – 150 ms

For the typical rock n'roll and country rock clean lead guitar sound a bit of short delay is essential. The mix is crucial for the playability of this effect.

- Delay   120 ms
- Feedback   10 %
- Mix   60 % dry

Setting up a tempo delay

Guitarists like Dave Gilmour and The Edge have created their own playing styles based around echo. If you want to play in time with a track and take advantage of rhythmic delay effects you have to know how many beats per minute the click track is. Use this formula to determine tempo related delay speeds.

60 divided by bpm = quarter note delay

divide result by 1.5 for triplet style delay.

Where there is no click track and no bpm information set the echo up by playing a note on the beat then damping it quickly. The delay time should be edited until the played note repeats fall in time with the backbeat on the track.

If you have a drum machine or metronome, try setting up a beat or pulse at 120bpm and use the delay times below. If you have a stereo delay then the triplets can be one side and the quarter notes the other.

- Delay left   500 ms
- Delay right   333 ms
- Feedback   20 %

Sustain

Long delay times can also be used effectively as a means of sustaining chords and notes. Use a volume pedal or the volume control on the guitar to swell in the dry sound and produce a wonderful wave of sustained guitar. This could easily be used instead of a keyboard playing chords.

Non tempo related delay and tape delay

These can be just as effective on the guitar as long as the repeats are not so obvious. One of the great things about tape delays was their low bandwidth which created a warm and sometimes modulated delay when the tape speed ran unevenly. You can recreate this on a digital unit by using a low pass filter on the effect, cutting it down as low as 4 kHz in some situations.

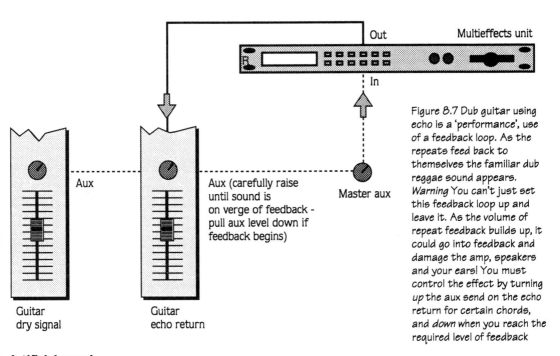

Figure 8.7 Dub guitar using echo is a 'performance', use of a feedback loop. As the repeats feed back to themselves the familiar dub reggae sound appears. *Warning* You can't just set this feedback loop up and leave it. As the volume of repeat feedback builds up, it could go into feedback and damage the amp, speakers and your ears! You must control the effect by turning *up* the aux send on the echo return for certain chords, and *down* when you reach the required level of feedback

Artificial reverb

This is a delay effect really but contains echoes that are so close together and complex in their reflection pattern that they merge into one long sound. When using artificial reverb it is often better left to mixdown because it's not easy to choose the right reverberation type for the mix while laying down the track.

Digital reverbs are most often used, and sound so good that for the guitarist the danger is always of adding too much effect in the mix. In fact the amount used is often less than 20% wet.

A simple rule can be used for general reverb:

- Fast tracks = short reverb such as gated and room 0.5 – 1.4 s decay. This is so that the reverb decay tail does not fall across the bar and blur the sound.
- Slow tracks = longer reverb such as hall, chamber and plate 1.4 s+.

Pre delay

Reverb also contains other elements within its parameters like pre delay and EQ. A rhythmic pre delay in tempo with the composition can give an interesting effect, and it will also provide stereo interest when panned to the opposite side from the guitar. Try it on short guitar stabs and pan the reverb to one side of the stereo. It's also interesting for chugging guitar.

Example at 120 bpm

- Reverb decay time   1.0 s
- Pre delay   120 ms

The live room

There 's nothing quite like miking up a stack in a live room but it's rare to have the space or the studio time to do so. Nevertheless, some reverbs have room simulations and so you can create your own artificial room. It affects the sound in two ways.

- Dimensions of the room – height, width and length. Smaller dimensions = shorter reverb.
- Type of surfaces in the room. This will affect the reverb EQ because soft furnishings like carpets and curtains absorb higher frequencies, and hard surfaces like wooden floors reflect them. You are creating a virtual room, as if the guitar was miked up in the live room of an expensive studio, when in fact you miked it up in your bedroom!

In metres a 14 (L) x 8 (W) x 5 (H) gives a respectable size live room.

- Decay   0.9 s
- Pre delay   20 ms
- Mix   90 % dry
- EQ LPF   8 kHz

The 8 kHz bandwidth restriction represents the fact that natural reverb contains very little in the way of high frequencies.

Density and diffusion parameters determine how complex the reverb pattern is. Some units like the ART and Lexicon series have an acoustic environment simulator which uses EQ to create preset types like tiled room, natural wood, club, and so on.

Of course if you want to get the Jeff Beck in a broom cupboard sound then you're going to have to change these dimensions!

Gated reverb
For special effects a gated reverb is an obvious but useful ploy. The length of hold is critical – too long or short and you can throw the rhythm. Also try a backwards reverb if you don't have a multitrack that allows you to reverse the tape.

Amplifier reverb
Most amps have the good old faithful spring reverb which is pretty low tech but I think can yield some interesting results if you are prepared to experiment. The low bandwidth makes for a warmer sound but its tendency to splash is irritating.

Pitch change

Pitch change programs in budget effects units are not that hot but can produce some useful sounds. They work by sampling the sound and playing the sample back at a different pitch alongside the original. For fine changes in pitch the result can sound like a sophisticated chorus and is excellent for strummed acoustic guitar and picked clean electric.

Use a stereo pitch change with these settings varied to suit:

- Left pitch fine   +10 cents
- Right pitch fine   −10 cents
- Left pre delay   10 ms
- Right pre delay   15 ms

Lengthening the pre delay to 20 ms plus makes it sound like a classy ADT and is great for lead guitar soloing, American style.

Heavy rock guitar solo
The limitations of the budget units are heard when you start using the coarse pitch change. For this setting the glitching of the pitch change will be audible unless it is placed back in the mix where it will still be effective.

- Coarse pitch   +12
- Minimum pre delay
- Mix   10 – 20%

Consecutive fifths and fourths

This sounds great for lead guitar but you have to take care when playing chords to avoid playing out of key! As the pitch changer is not being stretched to the limit you can also increase the effect mix level.

- Coarse pitch   +7 or +5
- No pre delay
- Mix   40% wet

Harmonies

To create musical interval rather than fixed interval effects specialised pitch changers like the expensive Eventide Harmoniser and the slightly cheaper Digitech are necessary.

Enhancers

Enhancers artificially generate HF harmonics from mid frequency ones to add extra sparkle to a sound. So for guitarists with tired old strings and dull sounding equipment it could be the answer for recording. It's a better remedy than reaching for the treble boost EQ. Even so, it's cheaper to buy a new set of strings, even a newer amp!

The enhancer is also used as a creative tool to add edge and presence to a good sound or enhance the stereo image with some phase shift. The trick is not to mix too much enhancement into the sound.

Effect combinations

Guitar pre-amps and multieffects unit combinations have a lot in common with studio equipment and can often be used without the pre-amp section as an extra piece of outboard for mixing.

Configurations

On a combined pre-amp and effects unit the pre-amp will be first in line, followed by the effects section. Often the pre-amp is analogue and the effects digital to get a better guitar sound.

Signal paths

Think of the processor as a series of pedals which you can plug in and out in a variety of orders. Some multieffects units allow you a large variety of combinations and others are preset. A mix control is often available for each effect too.

Figure 8.8 Multieffects configurations. These can be altered on most good multi-effects units

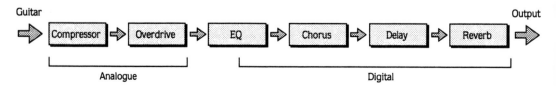

Modulated delay

Run the output of the delay into a modulation effect. If you are using a multieffects unit this may be an option on the internal signal path. The modulated echo will give a very big sound that is only suitable for compositions with a sparse instrumentation.

If you are not using a tempo related delay time try:

- Delay   450 ms
- Feedback   25 %
- Modulation   low speed
- Depth   to taste

And ...

Some effects do not have a studio equivalent – like the golden throat – but I suppose someone could invent something to emulate it without the side effect of loosening your teeth!

9

MIDI explained

You may be wondering how MIDI can help you when recording the guitar, but the truth is that it can be useful in studio pre-production, performance recording, and for recalling guitar sounds when you use effects units.

In addition, most studios now have some kind of MIDI equipment like a sequencer to aid the recording and mixing process. Automated consoles can use MIDI messages, and MIDI recorders control both the desk and keyboard equipment.

What is MIDI?

MIDI is short for musical instrument digital interface. If you break the title up into two parts it becomes obvious what this means.

Interface is just a fancy term for communication – like talking to someone only in this case musical instrument processors are doing the 'talking'. Things like MIDI guitars, pedalboards and effects units for example.

The digital part is the language that's being spoken. If we spoke digitally there'd be 0's and 1's coming out of our mouths because the digital language of MIDI uses just the two digits – a binary system. Fortunately we don't speak like that, but we used to communicate artificially with a similar system called Morse code. This old fashioned method of on/off switching is actually a good way to think of the MIDI communication system of 1's and 0's.

Cable

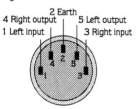

Figure 9.1 MIDI five pin DIN plug

2 Earth
4 Right output   5 Left output
1 Left input   3 Right input

MIDI uses a five pin DIN cable to carry this code, not a standard guitar lead. And no audio signal (sound) is being sent, just commands in the form of MIDI code from one piece of gear to another, telling it what to do. For example a MIDI footswitch sends a message to a MIDI pre-amp telling it to change patch. This could be a move from clean guitar to overdrive.

The cable can be a maximum of 50 feet (15 metres) long which is more than enough for most of us live, but in the studio a lead about six or seven feet long is enough.

The MIDI port

This cable has to plug in somewhere and that's what the MIDI port is for. It may contain two or three sockets:

- MIDI OUT – the 'talking' socket, the one that sends the message.
- MIDI IN – the 'listening' socket, waiting to receive the command.
- MIDI THRU – this is sometimes called the MIDI echo or echo back for a good reason. Like the MIDI OUT it speaks but it merely repeats any information that arrives at the MIDI IN port. It's useful if you have one master device controlling two slaves – a MIDI pedal sending commands to a MIDI pre-amp and then on to a MIDI effects unit telling them both to change to a specific patch simultaneously is one example. This would be called 'daisy chaining', and it's safe to chain up to three pieces of equipment together before the information chain starts to falter.

Soft THRU

When equipment has only a MIDI IN and a MIDI OUT, the OUT port can sometimes be switched to act as a THRU port instead.

Bad connections

Certain combinations of IN, OUT and THRU are not allowed:

MIDI OUT – OUT, THRU – OUT, OUT – THRU, THRU – THRU

These connections would be like two people trying to give orders at once and of course that never works! Likewise MIDI IN – IN would be like two people just listening and waiting – absolute silence where nothing happens! So it's best to have one person giving the commands, MIDI OUT – MIDI IN.

MIDI channels

The MIDI system is rather clever because it can send different messages to different pieces of gear at the same time. It's able to do this using a system of channels 1 – 16. This is similar to the TV where your aerial is picking up all the channels but you choose which one you want to watch by tuning to the right channel. In the MIDI system one piece of gear will be 'tuned' by you to receive one channel and the other to a separate channel. For example a guitar pre-amp could be receiving channel 1 and a multi effects unit receiving on channel 2.

Omni mode

Quite often when you buy gear it is open to receive MIDI on all channels. This mode is called omni, but it is better practice for the slave (the unit receiving the commands on its MIDI IN) to have its own channel rather than be open to receive any MIDI information.

What can you use MIDI for?

All programmable guitar equipment is now fitted with MIDI, so that covers pre-amps, effects units, pedalboards and even some amps and guitars. You could want to send commands for many reasons.

Patch and effect changing

A MIDI footswitch could be used to recall your favourite effect combination for soloing – perhaps overdrive with some compression and a hint of delay; and then slip back into a clean rhythm sound with a touch of chorus.

Parameter changing

A foot operated moving pedal can be used to vary individual parameters like volume, delay speed, or reverb amount in real time. This is a bit like the action of a wah-wah, which changes the guitar sound as you alter the pedal position with your foot.

Storing and retrieving information

You can download all your sound patches to a data storage device like a MIDI sequencer. You could then experiment by writing a new set without losing the originals and still be able to recall them whenever you want.

10

Using MIDI with effects

Types of pedal

Just like ordinary stomp pedals, there are more than enough MIDI ones to choose from.

Simple patch changing

For changing pre-amp/effect combinations in one step. The simple MIDI footswitch will act as the master, sending out a command to the slave MIDI rack unit. The pedal should have an LCD to show what number patch you are on, or about to choose. On the better ones this display will flash as you select the number patch you intend to move to and hold a steady illumination when you have entered that number. In this way you can 'hover' with your foot above the pedal just prior to changing the patch on the slave unit and make a smooth change in one stomp.

> ❖ **INFO** ❖
> *Patches may also be called program or memory locations.*

The advantages over normal footswitch control using a 1/4 inch jack are that you can recall the same patch as many times as you like, and it doesn't have to be an adjacent patch that you move to. With the latter you can just increment or decrement through the numbers one way.

Combined patch changing and effect switching

These larger pedalboards combine MIDI switching with individual effect on/off switching. The switches are dual function to save space, rather than having one set for MIDI and one set for effects. For example, you call up an effect patch with a configuration of compression, distortion and delay via the MIDI pedal. You then change the mode of operation of the board to effects, and can switch individual effects like distortion, on and off within that patch.

This gives you the chance to switch effects in and out as you would on a conventional pedal set up, rather than change patch every time you want a slight change in the guitar sound. Sometimes they use different MIDI commands for each operation: MIDI program change for patch recall and MIDI controller switching for individual effects on/off.

Pedalboards and MIDI continuous controllers

Boards fitted with foot pedals can control effect parameters in real time. This is achieved using something called MIDI continuous controller messages which send out data as you change the foot pedal position. Their most popular use is for volume, wah, pitch bend, and Leslie motor speed, although they can be used for many other wacky and useful effects. If you can't afford a pedalboard you can still indulge in some MIDI foot control by buying a MIDI foot pedal, or converting your faithful old volume pedal to MIDI using an Anatek MIDI convertor.

Integrated foot controller vs. rack effects

So far we've been dealing with pedalboards as separate foot controllers for rack effects. Yet, in an ideal world, if you intend using a sophisticated MIDI system with rack effects controlled from a pedalboard, it makes more sense to buy them both from the same manufacturer. The layout and command structure of the pedal will then match the pre-amp/processor. In other words if a footswitch is labelled distortion it will control the distortion on the pre-amp, not something else.

Taking this one stage further, it seems better to put everything in one foot controller/effects box, at the feet of the guitarist for easy operation. Many manufacturers like Zoom and Digitech now take the integrated approach with great success. There are no messy MIDI cables, no MIDI compatibility problems, they are easier to operate and visually everything is laid out in front of you.

Unfortunately things aren't always so simple. You might acquire gear as you can afford it, one piece at a time. And there's the question of choice. The Marshall pre-amp may have the sound you need, but to go with it you want the Alesis Quadraverb for its range of effects, and then a pedalboard to control them. This non integrated approach has the benefit of flexibility but a few pitfalls when using MIDI, as we shall see when we look at patch changing in more detail.

Patch changing for recording

Pre-production for instant patch recall

Remember that a program switching pedal does not control individual sounds within a certain patch, it just recalls a pre-programmed set. For instance:

> compression – distortion – echo – flange

So you need to do some work selecting, editing and storing the sounds you want for a song or live set beforehand. The time spent doing this is called pre-production time and if you can go into a recording session with your sounds ready to recall at the command of your MIDI switch you will save time, money and also impress the producer.

Patch recall vs. independent effect switching

The advantage over independent effect switching (like just adding a chorus for example) is that you are changing all the effects at once. Try and do this with normal foot pedals and you're likely to fall over!

Another benefit is that when you switch to a pre-programmed patch all the parameters, like length of delay time, amount of distortion, speed of modulation are right for the song – provided you've programmed them beforehand and stored the patch.

Practicalities

You can recall patches via MIDI within a song or between songs. The most obvious example is a change from a clean rhythm guitar part to a screaming lead guitar overdrive. Let's say that you have already pre-programmed this into your combined pre-amp and multieffects unit on patches 01 and 04.

Patch 01 'Clean Lead' might contain some compression, a hint of chorus, reverb, hi frequency EQ boost and a moderate pre-amp output level.

Patch 04 'Full Monty' has maximum overdrive, mid EQ work, some delay, a noise gate and a higher pre-amp output level.

Moving from one to the other in one hit enables you to get into solo mode fast with a completely different set of parameters. This is rather like a photographic record because you move from one 'snapshot' of parameters to another and then back again.

When to switch

Changing from one patch to another can cause problems for some effects units. Let's say that you're using a long delay time on one patch and there's no delay on the one you're switching to. If you switch while the decay repeats are still audible it will sound awkward because the delay will suddenly be chopped short. The same is true of a long reverb. This means you must switch when the decay has died down, or reprogram the patch to a shorter reverb or delay setting for fast changes. Even so, what you can get away with live will stand out as a glaring mistake in the studio under the close scrutiny of repeated playback.

Some manufacturers, like Digitech and Rocktron, have realised that there is a problem and have introduced effects onto the market with 'seamless' patch switching. These either have the ability to hold two patches at once, holding the original patch for a little longer, or have some sort of crossfade. However they tend to be more expensive as more memory space and processing power is required.

Real time recording and overdubbing

When channel switching, recording levels are crucial. Remember that it is the peak signal level that is important when trying to avoid overload distortion. So, for a basic recording you would need to check that the 'Full Monty' example was not going to overload the input on the desk when you switch it in from the lower level clean sound. On a more critical recording you are more likely to record 'Full Monty' as an overdub.

You may think that you won't need to use real time patch changing in the studio because every different sound can be overdubbed onto a separate track. Yet small studios won't have the luxury of available tracks so you may be limited to one, or two at the most for guitar. This means that

Figure 10.1
A A simple MIDI connection
B A more complex
arrangement. The pre-amp
and multieffects can be given
given commands separately
on two independent MIDI
channels if desired. To make
them change at the same
time both must receive
information on the same
channel, as in part **C**.

some real time patch changing could be needed. For the larger studio with more tracks, it's more a case of pre-production to save time and money.

MIDI – setting up

If you are using a separate pedal and rack unit, connect the MIDI lead from MIDI OUT of the pedal to MIDI IN of the slave unit. Check the MIDI channels on both to make sure that the information is being sent from the pedal and received on the slave unit on the same channel. Some units also have an incoming MIDI filter which you have to check in case MIDI program change information is not enabled. If that is the case, make sure that program change is 'on'.

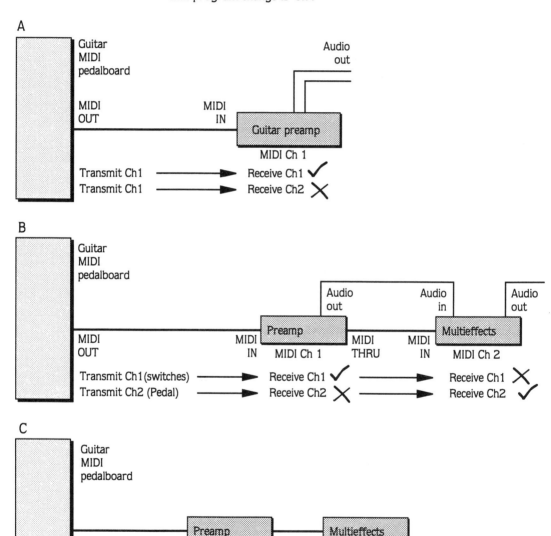

The message

Figure 10.2C

When you select a number on the footswitch a MIDI program change message is sent which contains this information:

> type of message – program change
> MIDI channel (1 – 16)
> program number (0 – 127)

Number nightmare!

The choice of a possible 128 patches is not random, but a result of the way MIDI data is put together. Although the details of this are not of interest to us in this book it does affect the way your patch numbers react to an incoming message. As you've probably noticed the patch numbering system varies from one manufacturer to another! And as a result you may call up a patch number on your pedal which ends up being one or more digits out on your slave unit. For example, your pedalboard is numbered 1 – 100 and your multieffects 0 – 99. In this scenario:

> pedal number 1 = effects patch number 0

So you're always one digit out! And if your slave unit works in banks of eight the situation will be worse. Yet help is at hand.

Program mapping

Many pre-amp/effects units now have the ability to change an incoming MIDI program number to match the number of your choice within its patch range. This neatly gets around the problem outlined above.

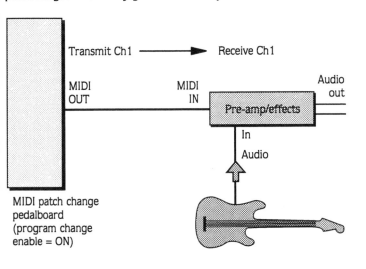

Transmit Ch1 ⟶ Receive Ch1

MIDI OUT

MIDI IN

Pre-amp/effects

Audio out

In
Audio

MIDI patch change pedalboard (program change enable = ON)

Figure 10.2 Simple program change operation of MIDI pedal

For example the program mapping table would be programmed to read:

incoming program number 001 = multieffects patch number 000

And 002 = 001 and so on through the whole lot. It's a bit of a pain to do this but once you have a program map it will be remembered every time the slave unit powers up.

Some patch switching pedals use the whole range of MIDI, that is, 0 – 127. So what happens if you're processor has only got 99 patches? Usually the slave device will go back to patch 1 when you hit 100 on the pedal. Other units with more than 127 patches (e.g. Digitech RP12) have internal switches that allow you access to higher programs.

Switch for bypass

If you have a rack mounting effect which can be controlled via MIDI but no way of switching to bypass, program a patch with no effect output mix. You can then recall this as your bypass.

Parameter control

Figure 10.3 Controller switching. On this type of MIDI pedalboard the switches have a dual function: either to call up a program on the slave pre-amp/FX using a program change message, or to activate an effect within that patch with a controller message. Note that the pedal can also be used to output information to change a parameter in 'real time', e.g. delay mix amount

Switching using MIDI controllers

When the pedalboard and pre-amp/effects are made by the same manufacturer, the pedalboard will have switches for individual effects on/off. Every time you hit a switch a command message is sent out:

```
type of message – controller
MIDI channel (0 – 16)
controller number (0 – 127) eg. controller 72 (distortion)
controller value (0 = off 127 = on)
```

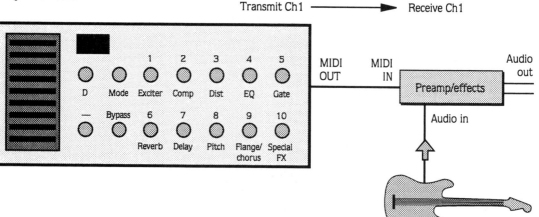

So if you just want to bring in chorus or delay without having to switch from one whole configuration snapshot to another this is a better method. Bypass is another function that may be operated using a MIDI control switch.

Performance MIDI – variable parameter control

This is one of the fun parts of MIDI. Remember that, using a MIDI controller pedal you can continuously change parameters like effects mix, pre-amp volume, and even individual effects like delay time and amount.

The message

Continuous controller messages are more complex because more information needs to be carried. For example the scale of 128 steps that we have been using up to now for MIDI is just not enough to tell a reverb decay time to move smoothly from very short to very long. We would hear the jumps in reverb time as we moved the pedal. For that reason more digits are added to the message which cunningly conspires to give us over 16,000 steps!

> type of message – controller
> MIDI channel (0 – 16)
> controller number (0 – 127)
> controller MSB value
> controller LSB value (combined value = 0 – 16,384)

Setting up

There are a few steps to follow but they are all pretty straightforward:

> Connect the MIDI OUT from the pedal to the MIDI IN of the
> processor with the MIDI lead.
> Check that pedal send, and processor receive MIDI channels are
> the same.
> Assign a MIDI controller number to the pedal. You have a choice
> of 1 – 128.
> On the processor assign a parameter, for example reverberation
> decay time, to respond to the same controller number you gave to
> the pedal. So:
> MIDI pedal – controller 11
> target parameter – controller 11 (eg. reverb decay time) - this is
> how the processor will know that the pedal will be 'talking' to that
> parameter and not to any of the others.
> Set target parameter range.

Range is the amount of change you want the pedal to have over the target parameter. It is usually thought of as a percentage so full range would be 0 – 100%. This is the equivalent of you pushing the pedal down as far as it will go from the off position. Target range is programmed on the effects unit, not the pedal.

Examples

Full range

For example. You want to change a reverb decay time from nothing to maximum using the pedal. This is easy:

```
set the reverb decay value to 0s
set target parameter range to 100%
pedal off (0 %)              reverb decay = 0 s
pedal full on (100 %)        reverb decay = 5.0 s
```

Limited range

But it could be that we don't want the total movement of the pedal to change our reverb from nothing to a massive 5 seconds! So we limit the range of the pedal action and confine it between a useful 0.8 s and fairly big 3 seconds. This will still give an impressive change but means that we can pull the pedal all the way back and confidently know that we have a normal, usable reverb with the pedal up.

```
set reverb decay value to 0.8s
set target parameter range to 60%
pedal off (0%)               reverb decay = 0.8s
pedal full on (60%)          reverb decay = 3.0s
```

Which controller?

There are 128 controllers (see appendix), but you can't fail to have noticed the bias towards keyboards, synthesisers and sequencers – at least as far as names go (modulation, breath control, portamento). Yet guitarists can get in on the act too because there are many undefined controller numbers to choose from ('undefined' just means they haven't got any specific functions attached to them and are up for grabs). So guitar pedalboards often use these or numbers with non specific names like:

```
controller 4       foot pedal
controller 11      expression pedal
```

Yet in reality, providing your MIDI guitar effects set up is completely self contained (i.e. it is not wired into a sequencer and keyboard system) you are at liberty to use almost any number you want! Guitar pre-amps for example don't have modulation wheels and breath controllers even though it might make life interesting if they did. So you could have a two pedal set up like:

pedal 1 (controller 1)   target parameter (pre-amp output)
pedal 2 (controller 2)   target parameter (chorus depth)

This makes life easy – two pedals, two simple digits. Yet, should you happen to be part of a bigger MIDI system, including keyboards and sequencers where there is even a slight chance of confusion, stick to the MIDI rules (protocol).

Otherwise you could end up adding modulation to the keyboards every time you push that pedal! I know that you should be on your own MIDI channel anyway but accidents can happen! So:

pedal 1 (controller 4)   target parameter (pre-amp output)
pedal 2 (controller 11) target parameter (chorus depth)

> **INFO**
>
> *The controller chart is orientated towards keyboards, but there are numbers that look useful for anything. For instance controller 93 – chorus depth. It is rare to find these implemented on guitar effects units.*

Using controller messages

As you can imagine when you move that pedal and all those digits start whizzing down that MIDI cable things begin to get a little hectic for the MIDI system! Some pedals have a built in delay factor to stop MIDI buffers getting overloaded but you should watch out for errors. If the equipment locks up the best thing to do is look for an error message and find out what to do in the manual. Failing that switch it off and after ten seconds or so back on again – this usually clears the lock up but you will have to work out why it happened. The cause is usually an information overload or error.

Examples

Expansive stereo delay

target parameter	delay mix
parameter value	0
range	100%
pan (dry)	centre
pan (wet)	hard left and right

Play one chord but don't damp it. Just after hitting the chord bring the MIDI pedal down quite quickly and listen to the sound go from being tiny, mono and dry to massively stereo with bags of sustain! If you can't pan dry and wet sounds in the effects unit it will still be impressive. This is also a really good one to try if you bow in the guitar with a volume pedal, using the guitar volume control, or via MIDI control from another pedal.

Expansive stereo reverb with modulation

target parameter	reverb mix, choose hall, chamber or plate.
parameter value	0
range	80%
pan (dry)	centre
pan (wet)	hard left and right.

Similar to the above effect but you can add spice by adding some chorus, flange or phase to the sound. This is effective running in line before or after the reverb.

Bright reverb

You're not limited to one parameter just because you've only got one pedal! For this you need to assign two parameters to the same controller number.

target parameters	reverb mix, HF decay.
parameter values	reverb level 20%, HF decay – low.
range	80%

For this I've included the range as a guide but you can set it up to taste. As you play a note or chord you will hear some reverb but the tone will be a little dull. Pushing the pedal down slowly you will hear the decay of the reverb and its HF actually increase at the same time giving a real lift to the sound. It's also great in reverse – from full pedal to nothing, especially if you alter the range to 100 % so the reverb all disappears!

Explosive reverb

target parameter	reverb decay, hall, long plate or chamber.
parameter value	0.6s
range	100%

Use some modulation with this effect. Strike a chord and then quickly damp it as you move the pedal from off to full. If you can pan it this is effective with the dry sound on one side and the wet on the opposite side of the stereo.

Selected slapback

target parameter	delay mix
parameter value	0
range	70%

The delay time needs to be short for this to work. Try around 120 ms with a small amount of echo feedback, then play a lick and bring in the slapback to emphasise the note of your choice. If the effect is not loud enough increase the range value. You could even have a small amount of delay all the time by programming a higher parameter value and then pushing the pedal for choice notes or phrases to get the full effect.

Classic Leslie effect motor control

target parameter	chorus LFO speed or Leslie motor speed
parameter value	LFO 10%
parameter value	Leslie motor speed – slow
range	100% (LFO speed)
range	30% or to suit(Leslie motor speed)

On the classic Leslie guitar sound as with Hammond organ some wonderful expression effects can be had by slowing the modulation speed down and up again for certain phrases. If your digital effects unit has no motor speed control then try using the LFO speed (effectively the speed or rate of a chorus) as a pseudo motor speed control. The range needs to be large for this because you will want to be able to go from almost nothing to a very fast. The trick is to move the pedal slowly as a real Leslie cabinet takes a while to get up to speed. Some digital effects units just don't have the range for this on the chorus patch so try tremolo instead.

On effects units with a speed control like the Alesis Quadraverb GT, you are effectively turning the speed from one position to another – slow to fast or vice versa. The effect itself then acts like a heavy mechanical rotating speaker system and takes a while to get going. The pedal effectively acts as a switch so it's up to you at what point in the pedal travel you want it to go from slow to fast. 30 % was near half way on the pedal I was using.

Rhythm distortion to lead

target parameter	distortion amount
parameter value	50 %
range	100 %

Volume pedal

target parameter	output level
parameter value	0
range	100 %

This is probably the most obvious use of the pedal. Even so you can play fancy tricks within your multi-effects unit if the configuration allows. For example if the delay section is completely fed by the pre-amp you can assign the target parameter to the pre-amp output and create swell effects into the delay from the pre-amp output.

Figure 10.4 Using a MIDI controller pedal to control distortion amount

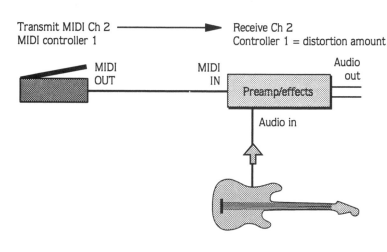

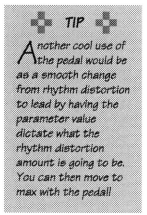

> ### ✚ TIP ✚
>
> Another cool use of the pedal would be as a smooth change from rhythm distortion to lead by having the parameter value dictate what the rhythm distortion amount is going to be. You can then move to max with the pedal!

Pseudo wah wah

target parameter	parametric mid EQ frequency.
parameter value	200 Hz
range	45%

You need a parametric EQ for this because the bandwidth (Q) needs to be a narrow 1.0 octave or thereabouts. The mid EQ amplitude needs to be a full on +12dB or more. Now as you move the pedal the frequency range alters giving a characteristic wah. The range is limited because above about 800Hz the pedal ceases to have any effect.

Narrowing the bandwidth still further to 0.2 octaves will give you an effect similar to a guitar going through a synthesiser filter

Extreme pitch modulation!

You may have noticed that digital effects really wimp out when you want to do extreme things with chorus. Pedals (especially old ones like the Electro Harmonix Clone Theory) were always much more fun. The following settings bring back an element of danger and spontaneity as you have to get the pedal dead centre for true pitch. The range allows you to move between – 50 and +50 cents which is extreme but doesn't quite put you out of tune. Try playing a chord and moving the pedal.

target parameter	fine detune amount
parameter value	50 cents
range	100%

It's also useful if you set the parameter value at 0 cents and the range at – 70%. Now when you push down the pedal the guitar sweeps up to pitch.

Pitch change

target parameter	coarse pitch adjustment
value	0 semitones
range	+100% or – 100%

This is great for lead guitar if you want to bring in a note an octave above or below. It might also be an idea to try consecutive fifths or fourths.

Options

- On most pre-amps and effects units you can program different targets for each patch. These can then be stored and recalled with the other parameters for that patch. So in practice when you call up your rhythm to full overdrive patch the target parameters are already in place.
- As shown in the bright reverb example above you can control two or more parameters from the same pedal. Obviously their action must be complementary. For instance controlling distortion amount and echo mix at the same time could be useful.
- If you are fortunate enough to have two MIDI pedals they can be assigned to control two different effects units provided they send out their commands on different MIDI channels.

Advanced patching systems

Session guitarists often have a rack of equipment and like to switch in individual effects, pre-amps and combinations of both. This complex task is achieved using a patchbay system into which everything is connected. The patching combinations are then stored and recalled using our familiar program change switching method.

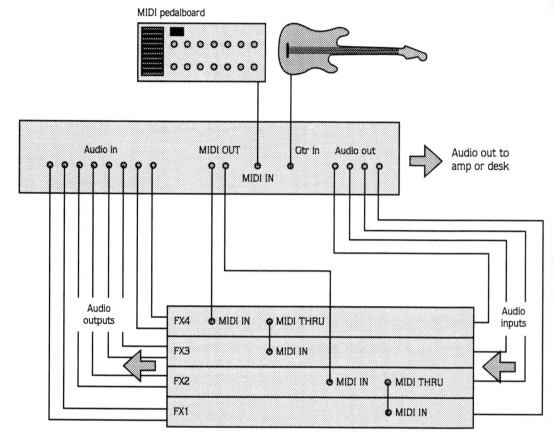

Figure 10.5 A complex MIDI patchbay system controlling, via pedalboard, audio input and output combinations plus MIDI of all the effects in a rack system

You could then for example use a Sans amp pre-amp with a Quadraverb and a Lexicon if you prefer that combination for a certain sound. Outputs can be fed to an amp or a mixer. A very advanced set up may even incorporate a MIDI mixer!

TC electronics have been operating a similar patchbay system as an integral part of their high quality delay units for some time. This is why they are often a popular choice for guitarists. On a smaller scale many guitar orientated multieffects units now allow you to patch in an external effects loop for your favourite pedal effect(s). This can be programmed into the patch as loop on or off and the patch recalled with a footswitch.

Storing and retrieving patches

Using a part of MIDI called System Exclusive (SysEx) you can store individual patches or the whole memory of your multieffects unit to an external MIDI recorder. All manufacturers have an exclusive MIDI code for their devices – hence the name. It also avoids confusion when you are sending the information in a system which has a few MIDI devices wired together.

Advantages of SysEx

- You can write a whole new set of patches.
- If something goes wrong with the device and you lose your patches you can still recall them.
- You can exchange patches from another guitarist with the same equipment.

The disadvantage is that you need an external device to store that data. This could be a computer based sequencer or a data recorder. Even if you do not own one you will probably know some one who will let you save the sounds using their sequencer. The sounds are kept on disk so if you are precious about your creations you can always take the disk away with you.

If you can it's always a good idea to store the sounds as soon as you buy the gear, in case of accidents. Some equipment fortunately has the ability to recall factory presets.

Method

You simply wire the MIDI OUT from the device to the MIDI IN of the recorder and put the recorder into record. The device ID and model number are first recorded, then the entire contents of the memory. The whole process takes about four seconds!

To recall the sounds your MIDI guitar effect must have the memory protect switched off and be connected MIDI OUT from data recorder to MIDI IN of the effect. Replaying the recorded data should then load the device with those sounds.

On the mix

Bearing in mind that the multieffects unit and pedals can be used on the mix, you can take advantage of their MIDI capabilities there too. A sequencer synchronised to tape can change patches, and real time controller information may be recorded from a MIDI pedal into a sequencer. This could then be used to control a synthesiser module or effects unit while the mix is running.

11

MIDI guitar and guitar synthesisers

Why buy a guitar synthesiser?

A good question, but one which is easily answered. The new breed of MIDI guitar synthesisers give you access to the entire range of sounds available using MIDI. So that doesn't just mean keyboard sounds like piano, strings and brass, but sampled drums, percussion, ethnic singing – anything you like! Can you imagine laying down a groovy drum track by picking out a rhythm on the guitar, adding the bass part on the guitar, and then some pad synthesiser chords, even triggering some sampled singing? It might seem mind boggling but it is possible with a MIDI guitar, some sound modules and a sequencer!

History

Guitarists have always wanted access to other sounds. Before MIDI came along there were stabs at creating guitar/keyboard hybrids like the Vox guitar organ (1966) and the Godwin organ guitar (1976). On both, the frets were wired to a set of organ tone generators and a string touching the fret completed a circuit to produce the corresponding organ note.

Unfortunately, the electronics took up so much space in the guitar body that the guitar sound itself was compromised. In fact until the late eighties the guitar sound versus electronics problem has dogged guitar synth production for one reason or another. Some models, like the ill fated Stepp DG1, Synthaxe and Yamaha G10 MIDI controller guitar dispensed with the real guitar sound altogether. Yet the most successful designers, like Roland and Shadow, have come to realise that guitarists prefer to play a real guitar with minimal modification. Hence the development of the pitch tracking pick up which Roland have fitted to their own guitars and eventually developed to fit most guitars. This no compromise design means that you can still play your favourite guitar, as well as trigger sounds via MIDI.

Things that guitar synths can do and keyboards can't
Some chord voicings on guitar simply cannot be copied on a keyboard without using other equipment. For instance, the mighty power chord of G. The middle G's are the same note but one is played on an open string.

Show me a keyboard with two slightly different G's in the same octave and you've found a strange instrument indeed!

A mix of real guitar and synthesiser together. Such as clean chords over a string patch. The guitar sound will add the percussive attack that the slow attack strings lack. Its bright, jangly tone will also sit well over the mellow, lower mid frequencies of the strings.

Expression. Certainly keyboard players have tried to copy this element of guitar playing. Subtle bends and vibrato on individual strings are the sort of things that make the guitar such an impressive instrument for soloing and melodies. In all but a few hands the keyboard is never as sexy! To make the most of this expression, the MIDI part of the guitar synth needs to be set up properly as we shall see later in the chapter.

OK. If it's that great, why haven't guitar synthesisers caught on in a big way? One of the reasons is money. They have never come cheap and even the Casio PG380 was expensive when it first came out. The cost of equipping yourself with a special pitch tracking pickup, pitch to MIDI convertor and sound module will still cost over a thousand pounds for new gear. Another just as important reason relates to the playability of the system.

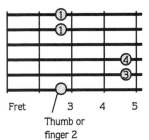

Figure 11.1 Power chord of G has two middle G's

Fret 3 4 5

Thumb or finger 2

Playability

The playability of the guitar synthesiser is directly linked to its Achilles Heel, the pitch tracking pickup. At its worst it can have problems determining what pitch a note is playing, keeping pace with fast playing, and imposing a delay between the playing and the triggered notes – especially on the bass strings. Thankfully they are now quicker, like the Roland GK2A pickup, but some change in playing style is necessary to get the most out of the sounds. We will deal with this in more depth later, but let's first look at the component parts of the system in more detail.

Pitch tracking pickup

This is the device that determines which note you are playing and which also has the ability to track vibrato and string bending with some degree of success. As the string vibrates the frequency of the vibration is measured to determine the pitch.

Pitch to MIDI convertor

This changes the pitch, now in the form of a voltage, to a MIDI note number and also uses MIDI information such as pitch bend and velocity for expression. A MIDI connection is then made to the sound module (unless the convertor is also doubling as a sound module) in order to trigger the sounds.

Sound module

Some systems, like the Roland GR1 are combined conversion and sound modules. Others, like the Casio PG380 have pick up convertor and sound module all contained within the guitar body! Most commentators agree that the system works best triggering sounds in its own module but you can successfully use it with external sound modules.

Most studio owners have some MIDI gear like a synthesiser, sequencer, drum machine or sampler. Provided the correct MIDI protocol is followed, by which I mean the right MIDI channel, amount of pitch bend and so on are chosen (consult the synth and MIDI guitar manual for details), you shouldn't have a lot of problems.

Figure 11.2 Three different types of MIDI guitar system connections. C is the Casio integrated system

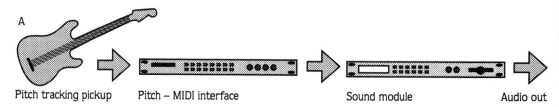

A

Pitch tracking pickup   Pitch – MIDI interface   Sound module   Audio out

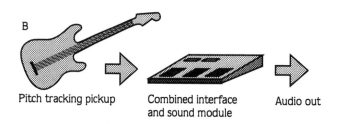

B

Pitch tracking pickup   Combined interface   Audio out
                               and sound module

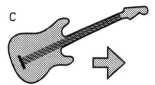

C

Pitch tracking pickup/MIDI interface/
Sound module

With a sequencer

Some guitar synths like the Roland GR1 have a basic sequencer. Even so, if you want to make the most of the MIDI guitar's capabilities, an external sequencer with a decent memory and editing facility is a better choice.

Connections

While the sound from the triggered device is connected to an amp or desk, your own guitar may be connected up in the normal way to your favourite amp or pre-amp with no compromise to the sound. On stage this would mean having two leads coming from the guitar. One from the pitch tracker and the other from the guitar itself. Some pitch trackers allow you to plug the guitar in and use its multicore to carry the signal to the convertor. This then supplies a normal guitar output for connection to the amp.

Setting it up

Unlike a synthesiser which has a fixed trigger defined by you putting your finger on and off the key, the guitar has notes which die away slowly. And its ability to be far more expressive than a keyboard means that the conversion process has more variables to deal with. The pitch tracking ability of the guitar synth is therefore the part likely to put most guitarists off. Notes may gargle, die away suddenly, change pitch – often jumping an octave, or be delayed. This sounds like a pretty depressing scenario but the quick troubleshooting guide below should solve a lot of worries when it comes to recording.

Troubleshooting

Some strings are sounding, but others are intermittent or not sounding at all.

Most likely causes are incorrect fitting of pickup or badly set up sensitivity controls. The pickup should be about 1 mm from the strings when they are fretted at the highest fret. Sensitivity can be individually adjusted for each string and those that do not sound or are intermittent should have sensitivity increased.

Some notes are sounding just from the action of putting the fingers on the strings. More than one note is being triggered when only one is being played.

Check that each string is passing over the centre of its own pole section on the pickup. If that is OK but the problem persists, it is likely that the sensitivity is too high and must be adjusted. If this only happens occasionally then more accurate playing is required.

There seems to be a delay between playing the note and hearing the triggered sound, particularly on the lower strings.

Because of the longer vibration cycle of lower pitches the string moves further and the pickup takes longer to work out the fundamental pitch of the note. Try using a transpose function on the synth module or sequencer to convert your notes by an octave or two down, and play on the higher guitar strings.

The pickup is fitted correctly but some notes die away or don't trigger as easily as others.

If there are any dead spots on the guitar these can affect the tracking. Play the guitar on each fret and try to locate the dead notes. You may have to avoid these spots by playing them on another part of the guitar. Another solution is to play in a different key and transpose the part. One commentator has even suggested the bizarre but pragmatic approach of using a G clamp on the guitar to change its resonant frequency.

Figure 11.3 Simple connection to sequencer

Pitch tracking pickup

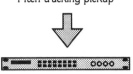

Pitch – MIDI interface

MIDI sequencer

Sound module

Audio out

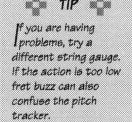

TIP

If you are having problems, try a different string gauge. If the action is too low fret buzz can also confuse the pitch tracker.

Notes jump an octave as they are dying away.
The fundamental note is dying faster than the second harmonic causing the the unit to track the octave jump. Again this is a problem with dead spots on the guitar. It is also more likely to happen with new strings.

Adapting your playing style
Not as hard as it might sound. Think of it as a change of technique – the sort of thing you would have to do when moving from heavy rock to funk for example. With the guitar synth you need to be more economic with notes and play cleanly with less accidental touches and fretting noise. Things that don't work are:

- Fast strumming. The tracker can't work out all the notes if they happen too fast, for too short a space of time.
- Fast runs. As above.
- Damped notes and chords. Can't distinguish the pitch from the percussive noise.
- Squealing lead guitar. If the harmonic is louder than the fundamental note the synth will attempt to pitch to it.

It's a good idea to play in the style of the instrument you have chosen
While you don't have to stick rigidly to this advice, it is important if you actually want the guitar to sound convincing as another instrument.

Piano
Piano players don't strum the keys! A pianist strikes the notes simultaneously for chords – something a guitarist can do by playing finger style instead of using a plectrum. You could also try dropping the bottom two strings by an octave to get that real left hand piano sound.

Sax, flute and woodwind
These are monophonic instruments when they are not overblown. Sax in particular is expressive and legato style playing with oodles of vibrato can help to capture the sound.

Strings and brass
Strings have a slow attack unless they're played pizzicato style. This works to the advantage of the slight delay in the conversion process – making it unnoticeable. Hence the tendency to expansive pad sounds from those early users of guitar synth on recordings! Another thing to note with strings is that you do not have to play the full six note chord. Often two notes are enough and for a cello you can transpose the lower strings by an octave if the pitch/MIDI interface allows.

Brass can be great fun, again don't overdo the amount of notes. If your synth allows, a slight pitch bend up to the note sometimes works. For brass stabs 'Township' style you may need to play slightly ahead of the beat.

Drums and percussion

Fast attack, short duration sounds expose delays in tracking more than anything else. Try playing on higher strings and using the transpose function to put the triggered sounds in the right octave. Using a sequencer or drum machine you also have the option of MIDI mapping the drum sounds to trigger from the higher notes on the guitar – in which case you won't need to use a transpose function. A quick listen to some drum tracks on songs you like and a glance at a drum rudiments book will introduce you to the style. Don't expect to be able to play all the drum parts at once, but you can have fun trying! And it might give you some good rhythmic ideas for playing lead guitar.

MIDI practicalities

MIDI channel

Obviously the MIDI channel between guitar and sound module must match.

MIDI mode

Poly mode is the best MIDI mode for chordal playing, but if more than one string is playing, pitch bend messages can get turned into semitone intervals. To transmit playing using the whammy bar, hammer-ons, slides and harmonised bending – lead guitar style, use the mono/multitimbral MIDI mode (mode 4). This assigns a separate MIDI channel to every string and therefore allows messages describing continuous pitch fluctuation to be sent independently on each channel.

You will need a multitimbral sound module, or a sound module capable of working in MIDI mode 4 (check your manual) to take advantage of this feature. MIDI mode 4 just stacks the MIDI channels up one after another, monophonically, and is found on some of the older synths like the Casio CZ1000 and Roland D50. However, most self contained guitar synth modules can do this, and most sound modules are multitimbral these days.

Bend range

The bend range of the sound module patch and the guitar synth need to match for the player to get the full pitch bend range required. Bear in mind the natural pitch bend range of the instrument you are triggering when setting this up.

Some guitar synths can be set to trigger changes in pitch chromatically. Basically this means that pitch bending and slides will track in semitones only. It's a useful setting when triggering some keyboard sounds like Hammond organ and piano.

Tuning

Many guitar synths are fitted with a master tune control for the sounds, and a guitar tuner so that your guitar can be in concert pitch. If they are not, when played together the guitar will be out of tune with the triggered sound!

Pedals

Pedals can be used on units like the Roland GR09 for special effects like pitch shift (parallel harmony effects), fixed rate modulation, modulation depth, brightness, wah wah, and hold. This last is useful when playing long chords and not wanting the notes to die away embarrassingly at different rates. You can also 'hold' a chord and then improvise over the top of it.

Velocity

Some sound patches respond to increases in MIDI velocity value by getting brighter as well as louder. This certainly makes instruments like brass, strings and flute sound more authentic. Check out the sound module and see if you can get the filter to respond to velocity information.

Recording the MIDI guitar to tape

All the information above will help make the recording process run smoothly. The actual recording itself is fairly straightforward.

If you are recording just the synth, the triggered sound, whether it's a sampler, drum machine or synthesiser, is normally DI'd through the desk. Effects may be added here, or the sound module may have its own in-built effects.

Yet there's nothing to stop you running a synth through a guitar amp or PA system and miking it up. This could work well for a sound like Hammond organ, or any synthesised preset you want to dirty up a bit with a little overdrive, like parallel pitch shift solos!

Bear in mind that sounds with a full range like resonant sweep chords sounds and bass synth may prove a bit much for some guitar speakers. A full range PA system or keyboard style combo with low bass and high treble will be more suitable.

The guitar would be recorded as normal and you would have to choose whether you record the composite sound of synth plus guitar to one or two tracks (sound modules usually have stereo outputs), or route the guitar to its own track.

Working with a sequencer

Many studios are equipped with a MIDI data recorder in the form of a sequencer, and this can be put to good use with guitar synthesisers. One of the main advantages of using a MIDI recorder over a tape based system is that you are not actually recording the sound itself, just the information that triggers it. This means that the data can be manipulated by the computer once it has been recorded. Bum notes can be put right, erroneous information erased, timing errors smoothed out and delays dealt with:

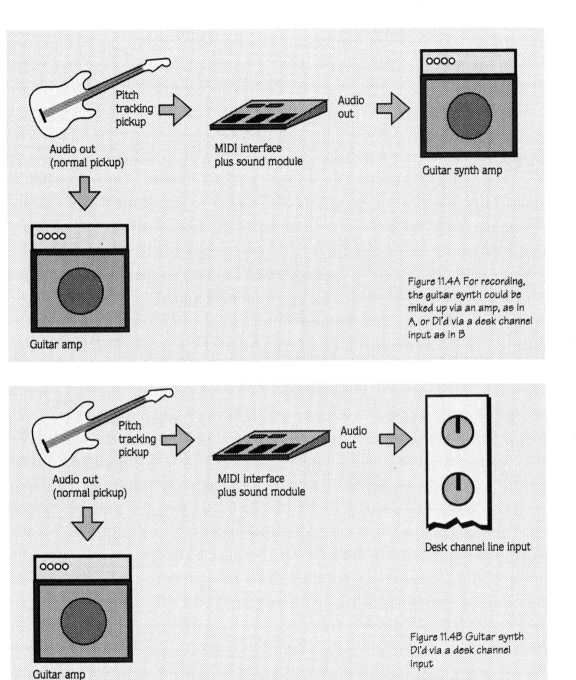

Figure 11.4A For recording, the guitar synth could be miked up via an amp, as in A, or DI'd via a desk channel input as in B

Figure 11.4B Guitar synth DI'd via a desk channel input

Quantise

The quantise function will drag the notes back into place if they are triggered late, provided they are not too far off the beat. A 16th, or Groove 16th note quantise should do the trick. Remember that quantise is also useful if there is no delay, but your timing is just a bit ropey.

Pre delay

If you don't need to quantise but just want to compensate for the trigger delay use this function. A pre delay of anything from 10 to 40 ms (dependent on how fast your convertor works) should drag the delayed notes back into time.

Timing

If you are having difficulties with your timing because the late triggering of the sound is putting you off, try using a different sound with a fast attack to do the take, then change it afterwards. Because you only record MIDI data, not the sound itself, you can change the triggered sound any time you like.

Transpose

If you play on higher strings on the guitar where the delay time is shortest, the transpose function can convert the information into the key of your choice, in real time as you play!

Mono mode recording

The sequencer must have the capability to record up to six channels of MIDI simultaneously. Most systems will record the information to one track if an original MIDI channel record function is available. The information can be split up later across six tracks for editing if required.

Remember that with mono mode recording you can also assign different sounds to each MIDI channel like so:

E string	MIDI channel 1	sampled breakbeats
A string	MIDI channel 2	bass
D string	MIDI channel 3	strings
G string	MIDI channel 4	strings
B string	MIDI channel 5	sampled voices
E string	MIDI channel 6	bells

In reality this could cause a lot of confusion if you try and play all the parts at once! My advice would be to overdub each section one at a time and use the polyphonic mode for any chordal and drum parts.

Unwanted notes

You can attempt to edit these out but it can be a painstaking process if there are a lot. If they are mostly short blips you can just ask the sequencer to delete notes under a certain length. You could also filter all notes above a fixed range out if you were recording say, a bass part. This would prevent some unwanted errors being recorded.

Re-takes

You very rarely need to erase any takes on a good sequencer because they have so many tracks available to record on. So if you almost got that solo in one, try some more solos on other tracks, then cut and paste the best bits together. This needn't involve any erasing of the original and is called non destructive editing.

Saving information

As with MIDI effects processors, if you have a guitar synth and sound module, all the parameters can be stored and recalled to your sequencer using system exclusive data.

In practice you are unlikely to record everything with your MIDI guitar synth – but you can have fun trying, and come up with some unexpected results!

Using pickups to get the best recorded sound

How pickups work

Pickups are essentially permanent magnets, usually made of Alnico with copper wire wrapped around them several thousand times. The steel guitar strings pass through the magnetic field and the movement of the string alters the shape of the field. This in turn causes electrical energy to be generated in the coil itself and is the source of the electrical signal that eventually ends up at your amp. As such on electric guitars it is one of the fundamental elements to the sound and is therefore an extremely important part of the recording process.

The shape of the magnet varies with the pickup design, from the individual pole piece magnets of the Fender, to the bar magnet and pole pieces of the classic Gibson Humbucker. The more windings the coil has, the stronger will be the signal. Yet there is a point at which the magnet can't get any stronger without having an adverse affect on the sound.

Both the main types of pickup found on electric guitars have names which illustrate their design or function. Single coil pickups have a single coil of wire wrapped around the magnet, but they are prone to hum when they get close to other electrical devices, so humbuckers were designed to eliminate this.

To that end the humbucker actually uses two coils surrounding two sets of magnetic pole pieces wired in series but out of phase with each other. The signal passes from one to the other but the interference picked up on both is phase cancelled when summed. The guitar signal that you want to keep however, is prevented from being cancelled by using magnetic pole pieces with opposing magnetic polarities within each coil. Cleverly the desired guitar signal is phase reinforced and therefore duplicated.

The strengths and weaknesses of the two most well known pickups are illustrated in this comparison of their basic features:

Figure 12.1 Guitar string moving in a magnetic field produces an electric current in the coil

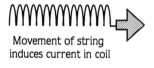

Movement of string induces current in coil

Humbucking	Single coil
Less HF response	Penetrating treble
Eliminates unwanted interference	Subject to interference
Warmer but with less definition	Clear, well defined sound
Higher signal level	

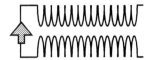

Figure 12.2 Humbucking coils eliminate pickup hum

Hum induced is cancelled because coils are wound out of phase. Signal is unaffected.

Pickup combinations

There are a tremendous amount of options available when wiring guitar pickups, and most electric guitars reflect the most usable options available. The classic five switch positions of the Fender Strat for example give you a wide range of individual pickup and dual out of phase sounds – some of which have become the trademark of guitarists like Mark Knopfler.

Humbuckers on the other hand, are well known for their big rock sound, but can also be made to sound brighter and imitate single coil designs with different wiring and switching options. A coil tap could be used to brighten the sound, and some humbuckers can be used as two in phase (or out of phase) single coil pickups. Obviously this will affect their ability to reduce noise, but it's nice to have the option if you have only one guitar for recording.

Recording and pickup selection

Many guitars use combinations of both types of pickup. A common set up is the humbucker at the bridge for lead guitar with single coils for middle and rhythm positions. Even so, for recording you would not usually change the pickup selection during a single take, but it is quite normal to try out different pickups on the same part before selecting which one sounds the best.

When overdubbing, a quick way to do this is by setting up the track for playback in the control room and getting the guitarist to play along to the recorded music. As the guitarist plays, change the pickup selection from time to time and evaluate the sound. As a producer or engineer the questions you have to ask yourself are:

1 Does it fit well with the sound of the other instruments?
2 Are there any parts of the guitar track which jump out of the mix because they appear too loud, or are too piercing?
3 Are there any parts which sound like they lack clarity?
4 Do some parts of the song arrangement sound better with a certain pickup selected? For example does the bridge of the song need a more mellow rhythm pickup sound and the chorus a harder edged bridge pickup selection?

Here are some of the answers:

1 If the sound is good you can get down to recording the part. If there are problems it's usually because the tone of the guitar doesn't complement the other instruments on the track. A quick example would be trying to use a bright bridge pickup sound on a track which already has keyboard sounds which are tonally similar. In such a case both parts are fighting for space in the same frequency area of the mix, and the result is a loss in clarity for everything in that range. The answer is to look for a guitar tone which is sufficiently different, and in this example a more mellow middle or rhythm pickup selection might just do the trick.

In complete contrast you may have a track with very little on it and find that the guitar sound just isn't big enough to work with a strong bass and drum section. This quite often happens when trying to use single coil pickups when humbuckers are what's really required for that fat sound. Other ways round this are to double track the rhythm parts or use EQ and effects to fatten the sound up. However it's best to exhaust all your options with various pickup selections and other sound at source factors like plectrum thicknesses and playing position between bridge and neck before you resort to the rest.

2 This more often than not means that there's too much harsh treble in the sound, and so a middle, rhythm or non coil tapped humbucking selection could rectify matters.

3 If the sound is not clear enough then the reverse is true and you should try the brighter pickup selections.

4 Big variations in sound level can occur for a number of reasons. The control of playing dynamics could be weak or the sound could be more resonant in certain voicings on the guitar. In either case some compression on the signal is a quick fix solution.

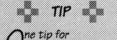

TIP

One tip for Stratocaster users. Watch out for accidental pickup selection changes mid take by guitarists who knock the switch out of position when strumming !

But there could also be another, more complicated reason. The instrumental arrangement of the backing could be such that there are more instruments working to complement the guitar sound on some sections of the song than others. When those instruments are present the guitar sound works, but when they are not there the guitar sounds exposed and usually a bit thin.

One solution is to use a variation in pickups, or even guitars, for different sections of the song. If you are short of tracks you would have to drop them in as you go along, making a careful note of which part of the arrangement uses which pickup. On larger multitracks they are more often than not recorded to separate tracks and sometimes bounced together before the final mix, or left separate for different effects and mix levels to be used.

Quick reference guide

Single coil

Bridge pickup

Light rock and country lead guitar

Pop and rock picking, particularly with pedal board pre-amps

Reggae skank

African

Overdubbing on keyboard based arrangements

Middle pickup

Pop rhythm guitar, especially when miked up

Rhythm pickup

Blues guitar

Hendrix and Floyd impersonations

Jazz (with some treble rolled off)

Out of phase (both combinations)

Funk

Lead guitar

Country

African

Pop and rock rhythm

Overdubbing on keyboard based arrangements

With effects

Because of the clarity and treble content of single coil or coil tap selections they are excellent when used with effects, retaining clarity even when quite a lot of processing is used.

Humbuckers

On guitars fitted only with humbuckers you are more likely to find two rather than three, although there are always exceptions. Like single coils, when you want to get a more mellow tone you move to the neck position.

Bridge pickup

Rock lead guitar

Chunky overdrive rhythm

Grunge

Indie

Brit pop

Dirty blues

Reggae lead

Neck pickup

Blues

Jazz

Coil tap and single coil variations

Reggae skank

Pop and rock picking and rhythm

Overdubbing on keyboard based arrangements

Using with a lot of effects

Vintage pickups and copies

Like the Les Paul, PAF's and early Fenders are prized for their tonal warmth, due to the aging and quality of the materials used. Quite a few manufacturers like Seymour Duncan and EMG offer vintage copies of the originals, some with magnets which have been artificially matured.

Active pickups

All the pickups we have been talking about so far have been passive. Active pickups include a pre-amp gain stage and have certain advantages when recording:

Pros

Higher signal

Better signal to noise ratio as less noise is picked up by the lead

Better signal level to pedals and effects

Easier to overdrive a valve input stage

Can be DI'd to a desk without having to use a DI box

Less prone to interference

Cons

The electronics that go to make up the valve pre-amp stage can themselves sometimes be the source of low level noise, detectable as hiss.

The pre-amp stage is battery powered and it can be difficult to change a battery quickly on some guitars.

Piezo pickups

These are more often used on acoustic guitars where the most successful location has been found to be under the bridge. A pre-amp, preferably with a basic EQ, is necessary to get the best out of the pickup, and the sound, as pioneered by Ovation, is a reasonable representation of the original guitar sound. As described in the chapters on acoustic guitars and DI'ing, the sound is useful in the studio as a supplement to a miked up acoustic or for running through an effects unit.

Some guitars actually use these pickups on electric guitars to give them an 'acoustic' style sound. I find some low frequency EQ adds to the illusion, but it's still more useful on stage than in the recording studio.

13

Sampling guitar

In my experience, synthesisers have failed to come up with the goods when trying to copy guitar sounds. A few of the great players like Jan Hammer can tease remarkable guitar style solos out of their instruments with the aid of an overdrive unit and some delay, but when it comes to clean chords and arpeggios there's nothing to match the real thing. All the best artificially created guitar sounds now are samples, that is, digital recordings of the real thing. Whether you're aiming for a realistic set of samples that emulate the sound of a guitar as closely as possible, taking riffs and licks off vinyl and CD, or digitally constructing a guitar track using digital editing software, you're likely to be using a sampler of some kind to do it.

Sourcing the sounds

Creating your own
You can create guitar samples from a number of sources. To start with you can start your own library of sounds if you are a guitar player with a sampler or have a guitar playing friend. In many ways this is far more satisfying than simply buying in one of the many sampling CDs advertised in the back pages of recording magazines like *Sound on Sound*. Using this method you can create some highly original samples, in addition to recording standard chords and licks.

From vinyl, CD or multitrack
Another good source is from recordings – your own or other people's. One or two licks lifted off a track and placed in a new context can be an exciting way to work, although legally dubious! Dance producers are constantly listening out for single riffs or phrases that can work within a new context and may even lift an entire backing track of drums, bass and guitar for a few beats or bars to create a loop for a dance track. A good vinyl collection of seventies funk is a good starting point.

The other advantage with sample CDs – even for guitarists – is that you get every conceivable combination of guitars and amplifiers that you could possibly want or drool over. From Gibson 335s to Fender Strats to Les Pauls using Marshall stacks, Fender Twins, Vox AC 30s and so on. All

INFO

If you're feeling less adventurous, then buy a couple of recording magazines, scour the back pages and take your pick from CDs of electric and acoustic guitars, country licks, funk and even Latino guitar. The advantage of these CDs is that they are usually well recorded, with the guitar sounds presented in a logical manner for sampling. For example, in fourths from bottom E up if you are looking to sample a whole guitar, or riffs at various pitches if you just want some slide or Shaft style wah guitar!

combinations which most people don't have access to. The best CDs give you a lot of variation, not only in terms of sounds, but also tempos and pitches with useful sleeve notes. Knowing the tempos is particularly useful when you're working with sequencers on dance tracks. It means that you can look for the samples which will synchronise easily with the backing tracks, which are usually running at a fixed tempo.

CD ROM format

Not only are CDs available which you can take into your sampler via the analogue input stage but CD ROMs are also on the market. The American guitar sound of Steve Stevens for example is represented on an Akai format CD ROM that is easy and ready to use for Akai sampler owners, but at nearly sixty pounds it's a considerable investment. A product like this comes with the sounds mapped out across the keyboard, and with loops and MIDI expression via velocity and aftertouch control already set, saving considerable time for the owner of an Akai sampler, but somewhat limiting if you like to program such things yourself. To take full advantage of this you need a sampler with a SCSI interface to load the data to the sampler, and most high quality modern samplers are equipped with one. For some machines it's even possible to load sample CD ROMs intended for other machines, but some tweaking will be required!

Figure 13.1 Left: rock band sampled across the keyboard Below: details of drum octave mapping

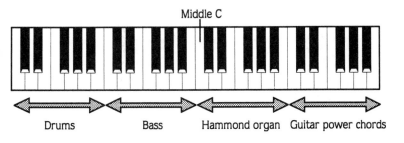

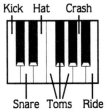

The sampling process

Input to the sampler

If you're creating your own samples the first link in the chain between the source sound and the machine is the input stage of the sampler. Most modern machines have microphone, line and a choice of mono or stereo inputs.

In the tapeless studio you will take the signal direct from the source to the machine, but in a multitracking studio it's quite likely that you'll want to take the signal via the desk to the sampler. This gives you the option of using ambient microphones as well as close mics, equalising or adding effects like compression, gating, reverb or delay to the signal. If you want to add these things later then record the signal dry.

Memory

Sample length and the decision to sample in stereo or mono is largely determined by the amount of memory you have in the sampler. Bear in mind that 2 megabytes of memory will give you about 12 seconds of stereo sampling and about 24 seconds of mono at full bandwidth. Sampling entire riffs singly is therefore a lot easier to work out than trying to build up an acoustic guitar multisample. A single riff might last only a few seconds, but for a multisample you may want up to 15 samples of the guitar at various pitches. This could severely cramp your sampler's style in stereo and still give you less than two seconds of each note in mono. Fortunately samplers can loop the recorded sample at a predetermined position to give the impression of a sustained note.

You should also consider whether the guitar sound you are about to sample requires a full bandwidth. For sounds like overdriven guitar and mellow jazz this is debatable. Remember that a miked up cab is already severely restricting the bandwidth via the speaker, so use your better judgment and experiment with different sample bandwidth – it could save a lot of memory. For example try distorted rhythm at 10 kHz unless you're going for a really bright fuzz tone!

Figure 13.2 An acoustic guitar multisample broken down into key notes and ranges. Adjust ranges to suit the characteristic strengths and weaknesses of each sample.

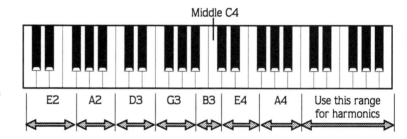

Pitch

It is less confusing to work with the sample at the same pitch as the key on the keyboard, for example middle C at the equivalent C on the guitar for chords and single note samples, runs and licks. This means that you don't have to do any transposing while playing back the sample. Even so, there are times when the guitar sample is the last thing you are adding to a multi-instrumental sample set of drums, bass and keyboards for example. If you can't match the pitch you can be sure that there is a real-time transposer available on most sequencers which can do the job for you as you record the guitar part into the sequencer.

Sounds that work

Some important points to remember are that sounds with vibrato, whammy bar pitch bend and modulation from effects will be problematic if you try to play two or more notes back on the sampler at once. Because of the way a single sample length varies with pitch across the keyboard range, all the above will occur at different times and different speeds.

For example a vibrato will be slower on a lower pitch note and turn into a warble at a higher pitch. For this reason, if you're planning to multi-sample something like an acoustic guitar, it's better to keep each note you sample even, with as little expression as possible. The expression can then be controlled later from the MIDI device that triggers the sound.

If you're sampling from a CD then of course your choice is limited by the way the guitar has been played and you choose something that fits the bill. Timestretch can be used, if it's available, to change the sample length without altering the pitch, which certainly helps when you want to play chords, but even this has a limited range on samplers.

Programming expression

All samplers give you access to forms of expression using MIDI and filters. The obvious ones are pitch bend and modulation. These you can set up and later edit if necessary to predetermined ranges that work best with the sound. It's nice to add a bit of vibrato to a lead guitar for example when the note is sustained. Pitch bend works for power chords and lead guitar, and how wild you go is determined by the range of the sampler and controlling MIDI device.

More complex expression comes in the form of velocity sensitivity and MIDI aftertouch. Both can be used to enhance the sound of a sampled guitar. Modulation for example can be programmed to appear once a certain level of keyboard pressure is reached, so you can let a note sustain and then bring in a little vibrato.

Tidying up and looping

Once you've sampled a sound you will usually tidy up the start and end points of the sample to get rid of noise and unwanted clicks and bangs. For multi-sampled acoustic you will also want to loop the note, and to do this successfully the sample should be evenly played with no modulation or constant decay. This makes it easier to find a section of the sample that can be repeated without obvious glitching.

Some samplers are easier to achieve good loops on than others, especially if they have a good visual display to allow you to find points of even amplitude. Some form of crossfade is always a useful feature too.

Dance track production

So far we've talked generally about sampling with some emphasis on making the sound realistic, but in dance production the approach to using samples is a little different. When doing your own sampling from vinyl or CD, the art of the producer is to pick out the killer lick, best groove or hook, and rework it into something completely new. This could be anything from two notes of guitar on its own to a couple of bars of a band groove complete with guitar lick.

In some ways it's better to have a sample that you can really work on creatively, for example guitar stutters using fast pickup changes and a lot of pre-amp gain on a chord make very effective breaks. Phasing samples is also very popular, as are wah and tremolo effects, although some prefer to use parametric EQ and filter control to produce these effects within the sampler. In reality you're only limited by your imagination when it comes to using sampled guitar.

Figure 13.3 Routing diagram

A Via the desk

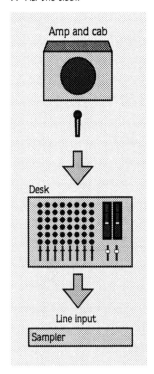

B Direct

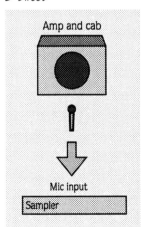

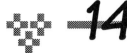

14

Guitar production techniques

We can't hope to cover all aspects of production in a book this size, but arranging and overdubbing are probably the most skilled part of the production job. Imagine the sound picture as an empty canvas that you are going to paint with sound. Everything must have a justification for being there. All the sounds need to work together to produce the effect of the whole picture. This ties in very much with the sound at source idea I wrote about earlier in the book. If you get that right at this stage then you never have to try and 'fix it in the mix'.

Inexperienced players and bedroom guitarists who haven't developed the skills that playing with other musicians bring usually don't listen to any parts but their own. But it's not just a question of getting the best sound or playing the flashiest lick. The best guitarist is the one who thinks about what the other players are doing, the style of music and gets a good sound that fits with it.

If you hear the studio expression 'sit in' the mix, it means that the sound works with the other instruments. There could be many reasons why a sound doesn't work. It could be too big: a Marshall stack would have too much bass for a keyboard based funk track. Or too small and light: a bright Fender Strat for Grunge? There are good reasons why well known guitarists choose equipment that is appropriate for the music both live and in the studio. But it's not just the tonal quality of the equipment, it's how you choose to play it. For this reason good chord voicing is a way of fitting your sound into the mix.

INFO

Only guitarists listen to just the guitar on an album. The average punter hears the sound as a whole.

Chord voicing

Because pitch and frequency are connected (remember, the higher the pitch, the higher the frequency), you can use chord voicing to improve clarity in the recording. Take the example of a band with two guitarists using similar guitar equipment – more common than you might think. Unless they are panned hard left and hard right in the mix, or given different treatments, it will be hard to distinguish one from the other. And how many times have you seen amateur bands with two guitarists playing exactly the same full sounding chords? If they used different chord inversions for a rhythm sequence the parts would complement, rather than fight each other to be heard.

For instance, if they were both playing the chord of A one could play AEAC# and the other A at the fifth fret position AC#EA. Not only will this give greater clarity but it will also create a more interesting sound texture.

Smaller chords
Just because there are six strings on a guitar it doesn't mean that you have to play chords with six notes in them all the time! Using less notes in the chord is another way to improve the overall sound. This is especially important if you're playing with a keyboard orientated band or on a session with a lot of keyboard overdubbing. Keyboards, particularly modern synthesisers, tend to have a very wide bandwidth and quickly fill the sound picture up. Many keyboard sounds work in the same frequency range as guitars too. You will find that on the guitar there is simply not enough room for big chords, especially barre chords.

So if you were asked to play a chord of G, you would probably end up just playing DGBG. This avoids a clash with the lower mids of the keyboard and the bass guitar. In effect you are layering the sound like a frequency cake!

Using distortion
Using barre chords rarely works when using distortion because you lose clarity. Thirds can also be a problem – Pete Townshend came up with a solution to that by using power chords containing only the root and fifth. And classic rock power chords heard on albums too numerous to mention are based on the E power chord which is then moved or slid into position for other chords.

Wall of sound
It could be that clarity is not what you're aiming for, just a tidal wave of guitar! This can be achieved by ignoring the above, multitracking the chords, and using a delay to merge the sound of them into one big mass of guitar.

Chordal dynamics
Knowing your way around the chords on the guitar is extremely useful. For instance, to create tension and a sense of build in an arrangement on a repeated section like a chorus, you can use climbing chord inversions. You may choose only to move from 1 to 3 but the effect will still be good.

Substitute chords
Varying a chord sequence by replacing one chord for a different, sympathetic chord can create a different mood in the music. You could add to an existing chord like Am by making it a minor seventh or an added ninth. Or you could substitute a major chord like G by its relative minor or dominant seventh – common enough in pop and rock. In jazz, chord substitution is an important part of harmonic improvisation. A good grasp of

Figure 14.1 Complementary chord inversions add texture to the overall sound

A major

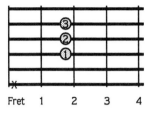

Fret   1   2   3   4

A major – higher inversion

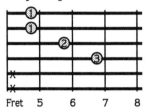

Fret   5   6   7   8

Figure 14.2 Smaller chord inversions may be needed when working with other instruments like keyboards

G major – full barre chord

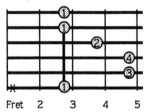

Fret   2   3   4   5

G major – smaller inversion

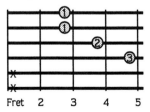

Fret   2   3   4   5

Figure 14.3 Townshend
chords A, G, B and E. These
chords are ambiguous (they
have no third) so can be used
instead of a major or a minor
chord

Power chords

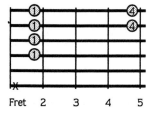

Fret   2   3   4   5

Use thumb for the optional low G

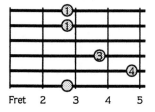

Fret   2   3   4   5

Use thumb or second finger for
optional low F sharp and B

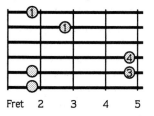

Fret   2   3   4   5

E – often moved to play other
power chords like D and C

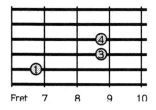

Fret   7   8   9   10

chordal theory is essential to add extra leading chords and substitutes which suggest and complement the melody.

Polychords and layered chords

The use of polychords and chord layering can be used to produce definition, heighten tension and build the dynamic of a piece when overdubbing. A polychord could be simply a chord with an altered bass note, like C major with an E instead of C bass – written C/E. It could also be made from the component parts of two chords.

A breakdown of the chord C major ninth shows that it has the component part of two chords contained within it – C (CEG) and G (GBD). It is both interesting and good fun to try playing one of these three note chords against the other as an overdub. And moving the chord voicings further apart might theoretically change the chord but can produce some excellent combined guitar sounds.

In much the same way you can overdub a chord an octave apart for an effect that is similar to a pitch shifter but has the benefits of real playing, timing and tonal differences.

Multitracking the guitar

Reworking a guitar part

One of the jobs of the producer involves listening to a part and suggesting ways in which it can be modified and improved for a recording. In a live situation you stick to one part, occasionally adding effects and playing lead guitar when needed. For the studio recording this one part could become several different ones. A typical pop or rock song with a picked guitar in the verse, chords in the chorus and and a solo could be reworked. Instead of using one track, in a pro situation you could use four or more to build up the sound and lend dynamic to the song. Notice particularly the addition of a double tracked guitar on the second chorus. Panned hard right and left this will really open up to a big sounding chorus.

Verse 1	track 1	picked guitar, clean or some modulation used.
Chorus 1	track 2	overdrive power chords
Verse 2	track 1	picked guitar (as above)
Verse 2	track 3	guitar fills
Chorus 2	track 2	overdrive power chords
Chorus 2	track 4	double tracked overdrive power chords
Chorus 2 rpt	track 1	guitar picking through chorus
Solo	track 2	overdrive power chords
	track 3	guitar solo

Chorus 3	track 1	picked guitar
	track 2	power chords
	track 3	fills
	track 4	double tracked chords

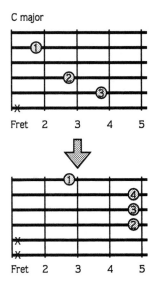

Figure 14.4 Building chord inversions on repeat choruses. The chord itself could rise, or an overdubbed higher inversion used, together with the original version

Double tracking

This means recording the same part twice and is very effective for rhythm guitar. Panned to opposite sides of the stereo the sound is wide, it leaves space for the vocal in the centre stereo, slight timing discrepancies lead to interesting shifts in the stereo image from one side to the other. If you intend to double track, your playing needs to be consistent to follow the performance qualities of the first take.

Tracking up the same part

This is basically recording the same thing a number of times. You will need plenty of spare tracks but eventually all the guitars will be bounced to one track. Timing differences on each will take tend to blur the sound but some interesting effects can be achieved. By the time you've done it four or more times the timing tends to come back together for a fat sound.

Harmonies

The effect of tracking up lead guitar harmonies is brilliantly demonstrated by the work of Brian May. All the guitar parts will be on separate tracks but on a small multitrack you will have to bounce them down.

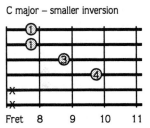

Submixing and track sharing

On a small multitrack you inevitably have to bounce down and combine tracks. When you do so make sure that your monitor mix is as well balanced as possible, otherwise you will get the levels wrong. Once guitar tracks are bounced you have to erase the originals to make way for different instruments, so the bounce cannot be done again.

Picked guitar	Power chords	Fills and solo	Power chords d/track	Bass	Vox	B Vox	B vox
Kick	Snare	Hat	Tom 1	Tom 2	Floor	Overheads	Overheads

Figure 14.5 Typical 16 track rock/pop song with some track sharing

Levels

Use the multitrack meters to make sure that the signal level is good as far as signal/noise is concerned. Don't use the meters for gauging the volume of a sound. You will notice that a distorted guitar peaking at 0dB doesn't sound as loud as a clean guitar peaking at the same 0dB level. The clean guitar will need to be lower to avoid sounding out of place in the mix.

Figure 14.6 Sub-mixing four takes of the same guitar part to one track. You may want some channel levels to be higher than others if it makes a more coherent or interesting sound

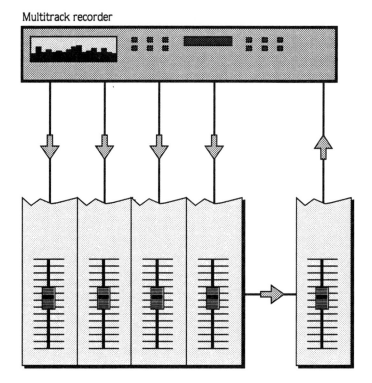

Multitrack recorder

Tape effects

Tape saturation

On analogue tape machines the signal level can be so high that the tape is saturated. At this point some compression and harmonic distortion of the signal occurs which can improve the sound of some guitar parts. The trick is to experiment with the record levels of your multitrack and check playback. Obviously extremely high signals will result in overload distortion of a non musical nature, even damage, and should be avoided. But taking the input meter into the red can yield interesting results. It's one of the things that analogue machines do which digital ones cannot. Hence the development of, of all things, analogue valve interfaces between the signal and digital machines!

Varispeed tricks

Most tape based multitracks have a tape speed control which allows you to change the pitch of the playback. This can be put to good use for special effects.

Real time pitch shift and modulation

Double track the guitar and on the second take change the pitch of the machine by a few cents either sharp or flat. When you have finished the take put the machine back to normal speed and listen. You will hear a wonderful sixties style effect that no effects unit can accurately repro-duce. You can even vary the pitch manually to produce chorus and other modulation effects although this can be a bit hit and miss. On analogue multitracks engineers sometimes slowed the tape speed down by touching the left hand (spooling) reel with their fingers! This produced some classic phase and flange effects like the classic *Itchycoo Park*.

Bright guitar

Another trick for analogue machines is to drop the pitch of the song and play the guitar part in a lower key against the track. When you play back the tape at normal speed not only will the guitar sound be brighter but your timing will seem better too.

Octave guitar

Used by Mike Oldfield on *Tubular Bells* the octave overdrive lead guitar was actually played with the tape speed a whole octave lower and then put up to speed. A curious mandolin like tone was the result. Especially good when layered with another normal guitar sound underneath.

Backwards effects

Backwards effects have been used on many guitar albums. It is a treat-ment that works for both lead and rhythm guitar, with or without effects.

One thing to remember if you try these techniques is that a reversed tape will also have the tracks reversed. On an eight track machine for example, what was on track 1 will now play back from track 8, track 2 will be 7 and so on. Be careful that you are not going to erase anything by mistake!

Backwards improvisation

Believe it or not you can get some great licks just by putting the tape on backwards and jamming along all the way through. On playback what were decaying notes will become bowed in effects, and a struck note will become a sudden stop.

Method

1 Fast forward to the end of the track
2 Reverse the tape
3 Record – double check that you have chosen the right track.
4 At the end of the track, reverse the tape to the original position and play.

Some parts will be good and others duff. It's quite common to just keep the parts that work and erase the rest of the take. With echo guitar the effect is even more extreme – try it!

Backwards chords

This is a useful production technique to provide a tension rush, or lead in to another section of the song (like bridge to chorus). Strike the chord on the first beat of the chorus but remember when the tape is reversed this will actually be the last backwards beat of the chorus. Bearing in mind that the tail end of the backwards chord will be heard before the actual first chord of the chorus when the tape is the right way round, pitch is a consideration. You could use the correct chord for the chorus, a leading chord, or if you are daring, a polychord.

1 Locate to the correct part of the song – in this example, a few bars after the chorus starts.
2 Reverse tape: it will now play backwards from a point before the start of the chorus.
3 Record a single chord on the last backwards beat of the chorus and let the decay die naturally.
4 Reverse tape and play back. The chord will pre-empt the chorus, giving a feeling of rushing into the chorus and moving the song forward.

Backwards chords using reverb

The effect is even better if you use a stereo reverb on the chord. The reverb decay can even be tailored to suit the tempo of the music and so control the number of beats over which you have a build up of sound. For example at 120 bpm a 0.5 s decay will last the length of one beat of 4/4, so a 2 s decay would last an entire bar. Often it is more effective with a larger decay tail – say 4 s. You can also try it with a delay. A delay time of 500 ms with 25 % feedback would work well.

Volume push

Another way to create something similar to this effect is to use a volume swell pedal on the output of the guitar. If you don't have a pedal you can swell the fader to tape on the desk instead.

Sampling

If you are lucky enough to have access to one, a sampler or hard disk recorder can be used to speed up things. Instead of laboriously playing and reversing tape to create the same effect several times you can sample one and then drop the sample in at the appropriate points. Rather like cut n' paste on a word processor.

Editing

No one likes to relive a poor recorded performance time after time. The bum note, the poor solo – we've all been there! Various techniques exist for making a performance up from several takes. This might seem like cheating but believe me, even top orchestras and bands have to do this to get the best take on tape for posterity.

For classical and other intense performances the most obvious method is to edit the master recording. You would play the piece several times, analyse it bar by bar, even note by note to pick the best parts from each performance. These are then cut at the appropriate points and stuck together to create the final performance.

A digital editor would make light work of this and would even be able to seamlessly cross fade from one section to another. Tone and volume can be altered at the joins to retain continuity. This method has the added bonus of being non-destructive and so if you make an error, you can go back to the original.

Tape editing is harder but has been successfully used for many years. A skilled engineer can quickly edit a piece by physically cutting the tape at the edit points and joining the correct sections together with splicing tape. Difficulties occur where a performance has obvious signal level or tonal differences where one take joins another at the edit point.

Multitrack editing

This editing technique can also be applied to multitrack tape where the best performances of a song or rhythm track laid down by a band can be used. This is a stressful experience best left to the professional, as your tape could be damaged by a fudged attempt! On a digital multitrack it becomes much easier for the reasons outlined above.

Comping

A more common method using multitrack is to record several takes across individual tracks and pick the best bits. For this you need a larger multi-track to have the luxury of space. Using desk channel on/off switches or programmable mutes you can select which track you want to use at a given point.

In sections

Another method, particularly useful for classical and other taxing solo pieces, is to use an overlap method on consecutive tracks. Either record the piece in specified sections across several tracks, which means you don't have to do any tight drop ins, or use an overlap method whenever a mistake is made.

This last involves monitoring on headphones and playing along with the original to get the timing right. A click track could be used, but many solo pieces do not sound good at a fixed tempo.

Again, use mute buttons to switch from track to track to create the final performance. Here a desk with mute automation controlled from a computer would be very useful.

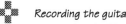

Time ⟶

X Mistake‼

Track 1	Take 1		Take 3
Track 2		Take 2	X Mistake‼
Track 3			Take 3 (alternative)

Figure 14.7 Using the overlap method to get through a gruelling piece without having to start from the beginning or attempt difficult drop-ins. Eventually a comp track will have to be made for the mix. Alternatively a steady hand or computer assisted mix will allow you to switch tracks when laying down the master

DAT with timecode

Using timecode to synchronise a DAT machine and a multitrack enables you to play as many takes as you have DAT tapes! Some guitarists like to throw a lot of ideas down and then pick the best bits. This technique has been used by U2's the Edge on recent albums and requires a special DAT machine that will lock up to timecode.

Dropping in and out of record

This is necessary when there is a limited number of tracks available, or when using a basic recording set up. It is a very useful technique for any engineer with strong nerves to develop! It can be used for repairing mistakes, or constructing a solo. Tight drops need split second precision but can be achieved on analogue machines wherever there is a small gap, say between two played chords or between notes on a solo. On digital machines you don't even need a gap as long there is continuity in the playing. Digital crossfade can take care of the rest.

Continuity

Along with the engineer's quickness of hand, continuity in playing from the guitarist is essential. This means keeping volume and tone controls in place, striking the strings in the same position as before between bridge and neck, playing with the same feel and dynamic and using the same pickup. You'd be surprised how many guitarists fiddle with the volume control as soon as the tape is stopped between drops! If there is any change in style or tone the drop is obvious and you just have to go back and do it again.

My advice is always to play from a few bars before the drop so that you can get back into the feel of the music. This means playing along with what is on tape before the drop in point and although it may seem odd at first it is something you just have to get used to. The engineer needs to hear what is on tape to time his drop in accurately.

Also, when the machine is dropped into record it will be cutting some decay from the previous take, so if you are playing along accurately you will replace that decay tail too. This is even more important when using sounds with long sustain created by reverb or echo.

On improvised solo drop ins, with or without echo, you will have to quickly learn the phrase you played just before the drop in for continuity's sake.

Lastly, when recording yourself, most multitracks now have programmable punch in and out points which you can use. Failing that a simple footswitch can often be used.

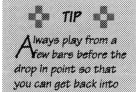

TIP

Always play from a few bars before the drop in point so that you can get back into the feel of the music

Playing in the control room

For communication reasons it is far better to play in the control room, especially when recording drop ins or developing a guitar part with a producer. If you are engineering yourself then you've got little choice unless you have a long lead for your multitrack remote control! For some sounds like amp feedback and for band sessions it's better to be in the playing area. But remember that you can also get controlled feedback from using the speakers in the control room.

Tie line

If you are playing in the control room you usually plug into a tie line that will link the guitar there to the amp in the playing area.

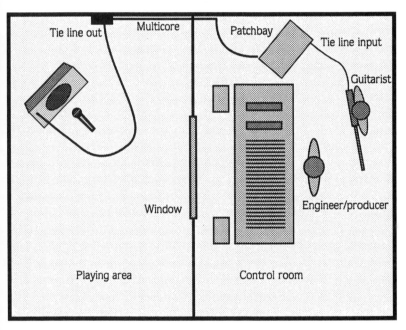

Figure 14.8 Studio tie line between control room and playing area.
1 Improves communication between producer and player when overdubbing
2 Makes it easier to quickly evaluate the recorded guitar sound
3 It's easier to play to the sound over the monitors than the sound from headphones

Different tunings

While it's common knowledge that slide guitarists often tune to open chords like G, it may surprise you to learn that guitarists may tune to Eb instead of E. This allows more flexibility and use of open, resonant notes when playing with brass sections. Brass instruments are in flat keys like the sax. Hendrix, Steve Cropper, Duane Eddy and even more modern players like Yngwie Malmsteen have used this tuning.

Folk tuning

Folk guitarists often tune the guitar to a chord like D, or even the more interesting D modal (DADGAD) tuning. This yields instant interesting chords and also a strong low drone note for backing tunes – many of which are in D. Rather than play barre chords when changing key a capo

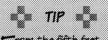

TIP

From the fifth fret upwards, the guitar sound with a capo is weak with very little bass end. However, you could overdub another guitar playing low notes to fill this hole in the sound picture.

is used to retain the flexibility and open nature of the tuning when changing key. So a tune in E would be backed using a guitar capo'd at the second fret.

Tuning and synthesisers

On a keyboard orientated song, because of the perfect nature of keyboard synthesizer pitch, don't be surprised if your guitar does not play in tune with some keyboard chords and sounds. It doesn't mean that there is anything wrong with the guitar intonation, but guitars, like many other instruments do not play in 'perfect' pitch all over the fretboard. You will simply have to re-tune a note or two by ear and drop in certain chords.

15 ❖

Mixing the guitar

When you reach the mixing stage, the console offers many ways to control the sound of the guitar.

- Channel faders control the levels.
- Tonal variation using EQ.
- Adding effects via auxiliary sends and returns.
- Stereo placement of the sound using the pan control.

Figure 15.1 Desk channels

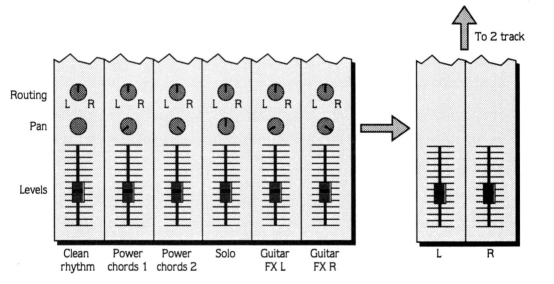

Levels

On large multitracks each instrument has its own track and desk channel. So for these mixes, once an instrument level is set there is little change in the fader levels if the piece has been well recorded. Some performance level changing may go on where extra guitars and solos are pushed up or brought down in level as the mix progresses. A good engineer will note when these fader movements must take place by reference to the tape running time or timecode unit and then apply them on the mix.

Desks equipped with fader automation can record such fader movements into a computer in synchronisation with the tape machine. Once recorded they may be edited if necessary and the information stored to a floppy disk or hard drive. This gives you two main advantages over manual operation:

1 You can listen more objectively to the overall sound on the mix without having to concentrate on fader movements as these are done automatically.
2 You can recall the mix at any time in the future should a remix be required.

Only the most expensive desks are fitted with 'flying fader' automation, but there are many other good systems available such as Optifile where the fader movements are monitored on a computer screen.

Budget systems

Smaller multitracks often have more than one instrument sharing a track and this makes mixing more complicated. However some techniques like channel splitting can be used to help (see below). Also while budget desks do not have fader automation, a great many of them now have mute automation. This allow channels to be switched on and off automatically using a computer synchronised to tape to record the information. It can be useful for mix decisions where:

1 You have chosen not to use all of a guitar take on the mix, but you do not wish to erase the parts you don't need. It is possible that you may do another mix which does include those parts at a later date.
2 You have used the comping method described in an earlier chapter for recording several takes and choosing the best bits from each track.
3 For splitting channels that have more than one instrument on them.
4 Quick tonal, effect or level changes are needed on one guitar channel. Again channel splitting can be used.

Channel splitting

Even if you do not have automation this can be achieved manually on the mix. A good example would be for a solo where the guitar has been playing fills elsewhere in the track. The level will need to come up for the solo and you may want to add effects and possibly even change the tone.

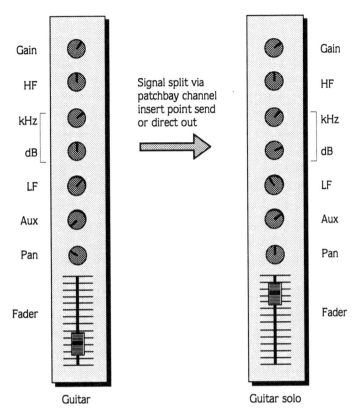

Figure 15.2 Split channel demonstrating change in level, EQ, pan position and effect send gain for guitar solo

EQ

If you apply the sound at source method mentioned earlier in the book, you shouldn't have to use EQ in the mix to try and compensate for a poor guitar sound. In a rushed session, or for a remix you may find that some remedial EQ is necessary.

Using EQ for clarity and separation

When it is difficult to distinguish one guitar sound from another, or from a different sound in the mix you could try using the EQ. For instance with two guitar sounds you could give one more treble than the other in order for them to work together. There are two ways to do this.

Guitar and bass guitar

There is a tendency for guitarists with EQ in their set ups to add lots of bass and treble. It might sound great when you are playing on your own but in a band mix this can fight with other sounds that have energy in those frequencies. For example, 100 Hz puts a lot of powerful bottom end into the guitar sound. But the 80 – 120 Hz region is also a place where the bass guitar is strong. If you want clarity between the two, some bass roll off in the guitar signal will be necessary. Some desks have a high pass filter set between 60 and 120 Hz for just this purpose.

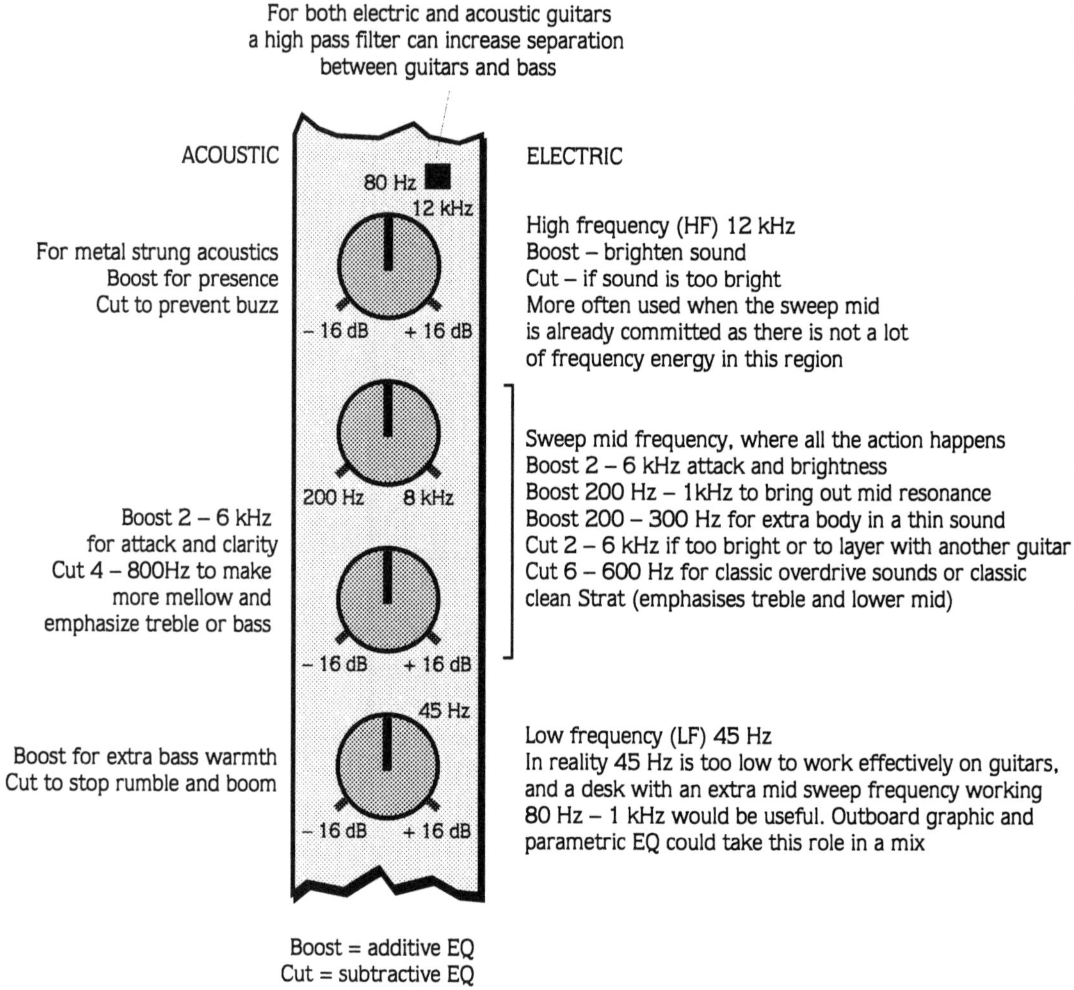

For both electric and acoustic guitars
a high pass filter can increase separation
between guitars and bass

ACOUSTIC

ELECTRIC

80 Hz ■

12 kHz

For metal strung acoustics
Boost for presence
Cut to prevent buzz

–16 dB   + 16 dB

High frequency (HF) 12 kHz
Boost – brighten sound
Cut – if sound is too bright
More often used when the sweep mid
is already committed as there is not a lot
of frequency energy in this region

200 Hz   8 kHz

Boost 2 – 6 kHz
for attack and clarity
Cut 4 – 800Hz to make
more mellow and
emphasize treble or bass

–16 dB   + 16 dB

Sweep mid frequency, where all the action happens
Boost 2 – 6 kHz attack and brightness
Boost 200 Hz – 1kHz to bring out mid resonance
Boost 200 – 300 Hz for extra body in a thin sound
Cut 2 – 6 kHz if too bright or to layer with another guitar
Cut 6 – 600 Hz for classic overdrive sounds or classic
clean Strat (emphasises treble and lower mid)

45 Hz

Boost for extra bass warmth
Cut to stop rumble and boom

–16 dB   + 16 dB

Low frequency (LF) 45 Hz
In reality 45 Hz is too low to work effectively on guitars,
and a desk with an extra mid sweep frequency working
80 Hz – 1 kHz would be useful. Outboard graphic and
parametric EQ could take this role in a mix

Boost = additive EQ
Cut = subtractive EQ

Figure 15.3 Most common
uses of simple desk EQ

Keyboards with some guitar

Keyboard sounds can encompass the entire audio spectrum from 20 Hz – 20 kHz. So where the song is based around keyboards and the guitar has a relatively minor role there is no space for a big guitar sound. Instead, lower mid and bass are often sacrificed on the guitar sound and some upper mid boosted (around 4 – 6 kHz), to allow the guitar to cut through.

Guitar with some keyboards

If you are using keyboards in a guitar orientated band, playing heavy rock for instance, the guitar strength is in the mid band of frequencies. This time the keyboards will tend to be soft sounds with a lot of lower mid and sometimes high presence so they interact well with the guitars and do not obscure the guitar in the mix. Typical sounds would be muted brass, synthesised (not sampled) strings, voices and bells.

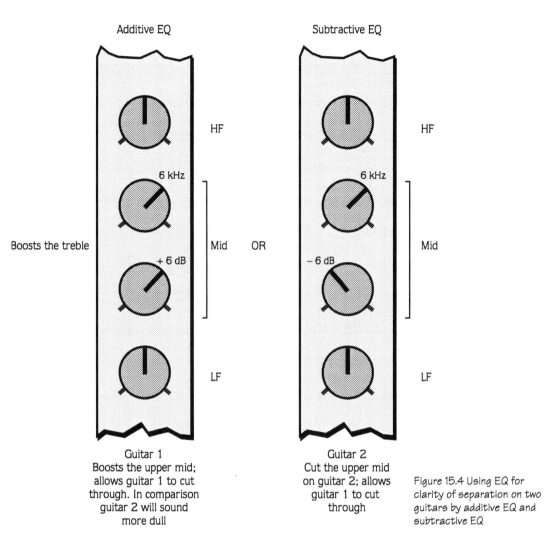

Additive EQ Subtractive EQ

Boosts the treble

HF

6 kHz

Mid   OR

+ 6 dB

LF

HF

6 kHz

Mid

− 6 dB

LF

Guitar 1
Boosts the upper mid;
allows guitar 1 to cut
through. In comparison
guitar 2 will sound
more dull

Guitar 2
Cut the upper mid
on guitar 2; allows
guitar 1 to cut
through

Figure 15.4 Using EQ for
clarity of separation on two
guitars by additive EQ and
subtractive EQ

Acoustic guitar

The acoustic guitar can do much as part of a band mix. It may be strumming along, providing a rhythm part, but it could equally well be starting a song off. Two different sounds are needed here:

1 Full bodied for the guitar on its own.
2 Thinner where the sound must fit in with the other instruments.

If the guitar take is all on one track the bass could be rolled off once the introductory chords have finished and the main track starts. Possibly even a little treble could be added too. But take care not to add too much treble because the high frequencies of guitar strumming can often sound like ride cymbal once it's placed within the whole mix. So if the timing is not extremely accurate it may throw the rhythm. This change of EQ could even be done by splitting the signal as shown later in this chapter.

EQ and FX

Equalisation can be added to effects return desk channels. Often this is visually easier than using the EQ on the effects units themselves.

It can also be useful to alter the tone of natural miked up live room frequencies where the room resonance is making some notes louder than others. Yet even artificial reverbs can boost unwanted frequencies in the guitar tone. This is especially noticeable on solo acoustic instruments where an artificial live room preset is chosen for the mix. To isolate and deal with the problem, solo the reverb return and check that undesirable frequencies are not being added. Use the subtractive EQ method described earlier in the book to cut these frequencies.

Using an amp to alter the sound

A common trick in the mix is to run the the signal to an amp and mike it if you don't like the original sound. The miked up amp signal would be brought up on another channel for the mix, or recorded to tape if you have a spare track. Some producers who have the luxury of large multi-tracks and lots of spare tracks always take a DI of the guitar at the over-dubbing stage as well as a miked up version. This way they have the performance of the original in clean form from the DI signal and can run it to an amp for the mix if necessary. Also, if the original amp sound was overdriven it might not work so well being re miked.

Figure 15.5 An insert send or direct output could be used to send the signal to the amp. A pre-fade aux send has the advantage of easy level control independent of the channel level fader. By pushing up the original DI'd guitar channel fader, an easy comparison between the two can be made. You might even choose to combine them for a mix.

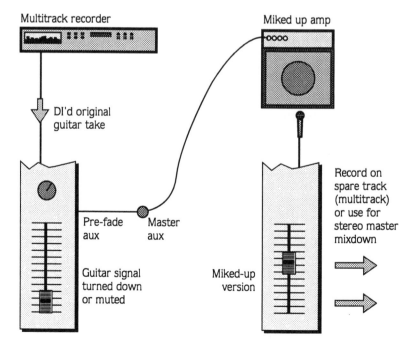

Using a pre-amp

Many's the time I've used a pre-amp instead of an amp to remodify the guitar signal on the mix. Adding perhaps some extra distortion or sustain for solos, or using the compressor and gate sections.

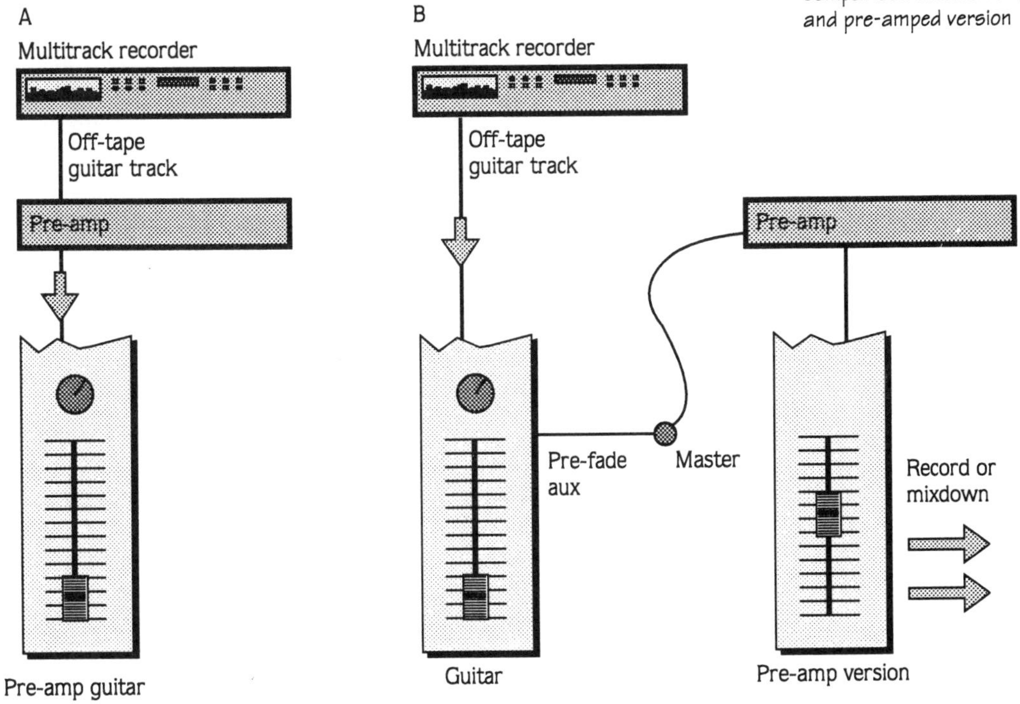

Figure 15.6 Using a pre-amp. The advantage of B is a quick comparison between original and pre-amped version

A

Multitrack recorder

Off-tape
guitar track

Pre-amp

Pre-amp guitar

B

Multitrack recorder

Off-tape
guitar track

Pre-amp

Pre-fade   Master
aux

Guitar

Record or
mixdown

Pre-amp version

Using effects on the mix

On the console the effect amount is determined by the post fade send and the effects return fader. Most inexperienced engineers have a tendency to add too much effect during the mix. So the question you must always ask yourself when adding effects is 'does the guitar sound still work with the rest of the instruments?'

A guitar may also be sharing an effect with another sound. For example a room reverb may be used to add spice to a number of instruments.

Post fade

As we have seen, it is the post fade send on each channel that is used to control the amount of level being sent to the reverb unit. So this set of auxiliary effect sends become like a simple mixer comprised only of volume controls. If you want more reverb on the snare drum than the guitar, then the level of the send on the snare channel will be higher.

The effect output, returned to the desk, controls only the overall level of reverb in the mix. This must be balanced against the dry sounds of the instrument channels.

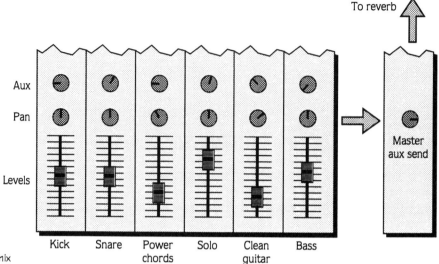

Figure 15.7 A typical mix scenario for different sounds sharing a single room reverb. The aux send acts as a mixer for signals going to the FX unit

To reverb

Aux

Pan

Levels

Kick   Snare   Power   Solo   Clean   Bass
                 chords   guitar

Master
aux send

Reverb

The amount of reverb level is determined by taste. In the mid eighties the fashion was for lots of reverb, now a much drier sound is in vogue. Overdriven rhythm guitar very rarely has much reverb added if you want the sound to remain raunchy and punchy, but for solos and special effects things may be different. Yet adding delay effects like these will alter your perception of the depth of the guitar sound. For example, a lot of reverb can make the guitar sound like it was played down the other end of the hall from the rest of the band!

Take an acoustic guitar solo. This may sound really good with a bright plate reverb setting of 2s or so. If you then add the same reverb to a strummed acoustic the first reverbed chord will be decaying by the time you're on your third or fourth strum! This build up of reverb will cause a loss in clarity and probably also throw the rhythm of the track as your strummed chords are continuously triggering the reverb with no let up.

✤ **TIP** ✤

As a general rule, for fast songs, use a short reverb decay time and for slow ones, a longer one.

Examples of reverb

Here are some examples to try. Remember that these are just a starting point and you should experiment with reverb settings.

Heavy rock chords
Some room, or no reverb.

Solo electric guitar
Higher mix of room reverb for raunchy track, longer reverb with pre-delay for ballads.

To effect   From effect

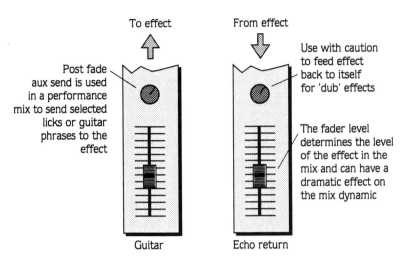

Post fade
aux send is used
in a performance
mix to send selected
licks or guitar
phrases to the
effect

Use with caution
to feed effect
back to itself
for 'dub' effects

The fader level
determines the level
of the effect in the
mix and can have a
dramatic effect on
the mix dynamic

Guitar   Echo return

Figure 15.8 Using echo as
part of the performance mix.

Solo acoustic
Plate reverb, pre-delay 25 ms+

Solo acoustic recording (no ambience mics)
Large room or concert hall. A larger pre-delay will give the impression
that the room is bigger. Some reverbs also have a listening position
(front, rear) and EQ to determine the acoustics. Start with 1 s reverb
decay time and increase to suit. Care must be taken with the amount of
effect you mix in against the dry sound.

Small room, ambient mics
On electric or acoustic guitar you can increase the apparent size of the
room by adding artificial reverb to the real room mics. A Room reverb of
0.8 s – 1.6 s should be suitable.

Using delay

Again, this may be on a shared send with vocals for example. But if you
can spare a delay effect just for guitar it is a lot easier to mix. Long delays
are often used for solos but can also be applied to rhythm guitar to create
the 'wall of guitar' sound, or to blend guitar into other instruments in the
song. It's also nice to catch individual guitar phrases by doing a bit of performance mixing. This involves bringing up the level of the effects return
for the favoured lick, or just sending that lick to the effect by turning up
the effects send at the appropriate moment.

Other delay effects mentioned in the chapter on effects may be used
but remember that they will place the guitar sound further back in the
mix. That is, they will make it sound further away. Sometimes this can be
used to separate the sound from another similar one if there is not
enough clarity in the mix.

Figure 15.9 Comp ducking the guitar level. The amount of gain reduction is determined by the threshold and ratio settings, and the speed of the guitar level changes by the attack and release controls

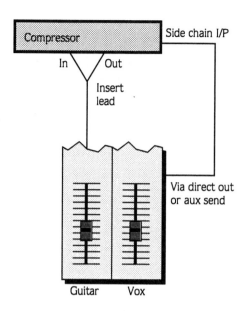

Compression

Even if you have used some when overdubbing you may need more for the mix. Its function is twofold.

> 1 To smooth unwanted signal peaks
> 2 To maintain an average signal level that will make the whole guitar track sound louder.

It's not uncommon for some compression to be applied to the whole mix, sometimes in addition to individual instrument compression. But remember that it will increase background noise, and for every 1dB of gain reduction, that's 1dB lessening of the signal/noise ratio!

Side chain the compressor

One mixing trick involving compression is for times when the guitar level seems to be swamping the vocal but you like the high guitar level in the gaps between the sung lines. Run the guitar through a compressor and the vocal to the side chain of the compressor. This allows the vocal to control the volume of the guitar automatically. When there is singing the compressor turns the guitar level down by applying gain reduction. When there is no singing the guitar level returns to normal. The amount of gain reduction is determined by the threshold and ratio settings, and the speed of the guitar level changes by the attack and release controls.

Guitar multieffects

Remember that you can use the effects in a combined guitar pre-amp/multieffects unit on the mix. On some, like the Alesis Quadraverb GT the pre-amp can actually be bypassed if you just want to use the effects section.

Stereo placement

Let's look at some typical mix scenarios.

Solo acoustic instrument

You could have four or more tracks to deal with here, and possibly some effects return channels. The two close guitar mics would not be panned wide because this would give a totally unrealistic width to the instrument! In contrast the stereo reverb, or room ambience mics can be panned wide if you wish.

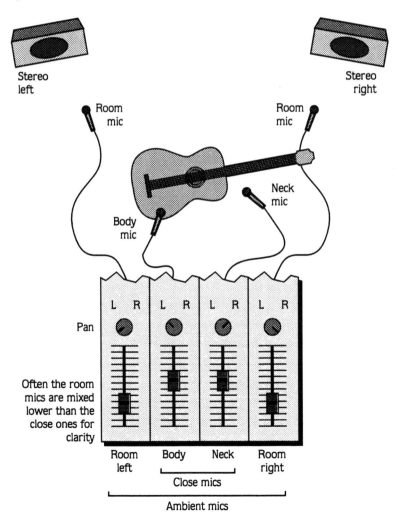

Figure 15.10 Mixing a solo acoustic. The room mics increase stereo width, because of their pan position, and depth of image, because they are further from the sound source and pick up the room's reflected sound. Try and build a natural sound 'picture' when you mix. The close mics should have a narrower stereo image than the room mics if you want to accurately reconstruct the original sound in a stereo mix

As part of a band

Many classic albums featuring two guitarists use panning to separate the sounds. One is sent to stereo left and one to stereo right. The same approach could be used for guitar and keyboards.

Figure 15.11 Separation improves clarity and stereo interest between two guitars or guitar and keyboard

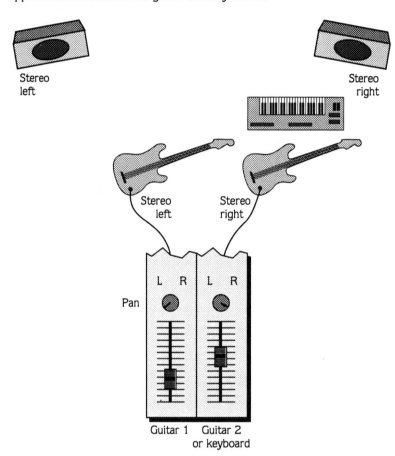

The 'on stage' mix

For a band you could take the band 'on stage' approach to get something approaching a natural mix. It is a technique applied to rock bands by excellent mix engineers like Bob Clearmountain. Imagine the guitar on stage and where the musicians would be positioned.

Complex mixes

For a more complicated mix using several overdubbed guitars, the panning will be used for sound separation and for the rhythmic effect of one guitar playing off against another. It's also quite effective to have a simple mix for a song verse and a bigger mix for the chorus.

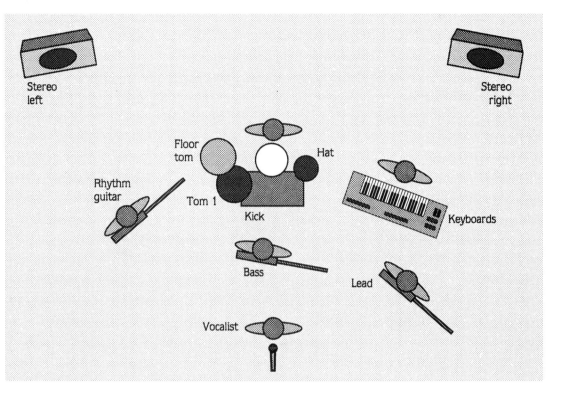

Figure 15.12 The 'on-stage' mix approach to stereo placement

Mute as noise gate

You really need a programmable mute for this. if you do not have a noise gate you can switch the channel off when the guitar is not playing. Unfortunately this is an on/off gate and has no decay time to follow the natural decay of the guitar, so care is needed. I would suggest using an external single ended noise reduction system for guitar.

It is surprising how much noise you can get away with on a rock recording once all the instruments are playing. The weak points are before the track starts and ends, and areas of sparse instrumentation which do not mask the noise. It is good practice to mute channels when they are not being used and when the instrument is not playing. For some a little amp hiss and guitar noise adds to the excitement and providing it does not dominate you can leave it in. Steve Vai for instance leaves noise natural to the electric instrument on the mix where others might take it out.

Don't just mix the guitar!

All the above may be used to improve clarity, but the most important thing to remember when doing a mix is not just to listen to the guitar. You might not feel like it but the other instruments have just as important a role to play in the way the whole composition sounds. The guitar's chance to shine most obviously is when it is the featured instrument, like on a guitar solo. In other sections of the song it may be playing an equally important supportive role.

Appendix – General MIDI

General MIDI drum map

		Standard set	Brush set	Orch. set			Standard set	Brush set	Orch. set
D#0	27	high Q	Sound FX	Closed hat	B2	59	Ride cymbal 2		
E0	28	Slap	Sound FX	Pedal hat	C3	60	Hi bongo		
F0	29	Scratch push	Sound FX	Open hat	C#3	61	Lo bongo		
F#0	30	Scratch pull	Sound FX	Ride cymb	D3	62	Conga slap		
G0	31	Sticks			D#3	63	Conga hi		
G#0	32	Square click		Sound FX	E3	64	Conga lo		
A0	33	Metronome click	Sound FX		F3	65	Timbale hi		
A#0	34	Metronome bell	Sound FX		F#3	66	Timbale lo		
B0	35	Kick drum 2		Concert BD2	G3	67	Go go bell hi		
C1	36	Kick drum 1		Concert BD1*	G#3	68	Go go bell lo		
C#1	37	Sidestick			A3	69	Cabasa		
D1	38	Snare drum 1	Brush tap	Concert SD	A#3	70	Maracas		
D#1	39	Hand claps	Brush slap	Castanets	B3	71	Whistle short		
E1	40	Snare drum 2	Brush swirl	Concert SD	C4	72	Whistle long		
F1	41	Lo tom 2		Timpani F	C#4	73	Short guiro		
F#1	42	closed hat		Timpani F#	D4	74	Long guiro		
G1	43	Lo tom 1		Timpani G	D#4	75	Claves		
G#1	44	Pedal hat		Timpani G#	E4	76	Hi woodblock		
A1	45	Mid tom 2		Timpani A	F4	77	Lo woodblock		
A#1	46	Open hat		Timpani A#	F#4	78	Mute quica		
B1	47	Mid tom		Timpani B	G4	79	Open quica		
C2	48	Hi tom 2		Timpani C	G#4	80	Mute triangle		
C#2	49	Crash cymbal		Timpani C#	A4	81	Open triangle		
D2	50	Hi tom 1		Timpani D	A#4	82	Shaker		
D#2	51	Ride cymbal		Timpani D#	B4	83	Sleighbells		
E2	52	Chinese cymbal		Timpani E	C5	84	Castanets		
F2	53	Ride bell		Timpani F	C#5	85	Mute surdo		
F#2	54	Tambourine			D5	86	Open surdo		
G2	55	Splash cymbal			D#5	87			
G#2	56	Cow bell			E5	88	Applause		
A2	57	Crash cymbal 2		Concert cymb2					
A#2	58	Quijada		Concert cymb1					

General MIDI program change numbers

Prog	Name	Prog	Name	Prog	Name
000	Piano 1	043	Contrabass	086	5th saw wave
001	Piano 2	044	Tremolo strings	087	Bass and lead
002	Piano 3	045	Pizzicatto strings	088	Fantasia
003	Honky tonk	046	Harp	089	Warm pad
004	E. piano 1	047	Timpani	090	Polysynth
005	E. piano 2	048	Strings	091	Space voice
006	Harpsichord	049	Slo strings	092	Bowed glass
007	Clav	050	Synth strings 1	093	Metal pad
008	Celesta	051	Synth strings 2	094	Halo pad
009	Glockenspiel	052	Choir aahs	095	Sweep pad
010	Music box	053	Voice oohs	096	Ice rain
011	Vibraphone	054	Synth vox	097	Soundtrack
012	Marimba	055	Orchestra hit	098	Crystal
013	Xylophone	056	Trumpet	099	Atmosphere
014	Tubular bells	057	Trombone	100	Brightness
015	Santur	058	Tuba	101	Goblin
016	Organ 1	059	Muted trumpet	102	Echo drops
017	Organ 2	060	French horn	103	Star theme
018	Organ 3	061	Brass 1	104	Sitar
019	Church organ 1	062	Synth brass 1	105	Banjo
020	Reed organ	063	Synth brass 2	106	Shamisen
021	French accordion	064	Soprano sax	107	Koto
022	Harmonica	065	Alto sax	108	Kalimba
023	Bandneon	066	Tenor sax	109	Bagpipe
024	Nylon strung guitar	067	Baritone sax	110	Fiddle
025	Steel strung guitar	068	Oboe	111	Shannai
026	Jazz guitar	069	English horn	112	Tinkle bell
027	Clean guitar	070	Bassoon	113	Agogo
028	Muted guitar	071	Clarinet	114	Steel drums
029	Overdrive guitar	072	Piccolo	115	Woodblock
030	Distortion guitar	073	Flute	116	Taiko
031	Guitar harmonics	074	Recorder	117	Melo tom 1
032	Acoustic bass	075	Pan flute	118	Synth drum
033	Fingered bass	076	Bottle blow	119	Reverse cymbal
034	Picked bass	077	Shakuhachi	120	Guitar fret noise
035	Fretless bass	078	Whistle	121	Fl.Key click
036	Slap bass 1	079	Ocarina	122	Seashore
037	Slap bass 2	080	Square wave	123	Bird
038	Synth bass 1	081	Saw wave	124	Telephone 1
039	Synth bass 2	082	Synth calliope	125	Helicopter
040	Violin	083	Chiffer lead	126	Applause
041	Viola	084	Charang	127	Gun shot
042	Cello	085	Solo vox		

General MIDI control change numbers

Control no.	Function	Control no.	Function
0	Bank select	75	Undefined/reverb
1	Modulation wheel	76	Undefined/delay
2	Breath controller	77	Undefined/pitch transposer
3	Undefined	78	Undefined/flange or chorus
4	Foot controller	79	Undefined/special effects
5	Portamento time	80 – 83	General purpose 5-8
6	Data entry	84	Portamento control
7	Main volume	85 – 90	Undefined
8	Balance	91	Effects depth (effect 1)
9	Undefined	92	Tremolo depth (effect 2)
10	Pan	93	Chorus depth (effect 3)
11	Expression	94	Celeste depth (effect 4)
12	Effect control 1	95	Phaser depth (effect 5)
13	Effect control 2	96	Data increment
14 – 15	Undefined	97	Data decrement
16 – 19	General purpose 1-4	98	Non-registered parameter no. LSB
20 – 31	Undefined	99	Non-registered parameter no.MSB
32 – 63	LSB for control changes 0 – 31	100	Registered parameter no. LSB
64	Damper/sustain pedal	101	Registered parameter no. MSB
65	Portamento	102 – 119	Undefined
66	Sostenuto	120	All sound off
67	Soft pedal	121	Reset all controllers
68	Legato footswitch	122	Local control
69	Hold 2	123	All notes off
70	Sound variation/exciter	124	Omni mode off
71	Harmonic content/compressor	125	Omni mode on
72	Release time/distortion	126	Mono mode on
73	Attack time/equaliser	127	Poly mode on
74	Brightness/expander or noise gate		

Index